VICTIM OF MY

OWN MIND

Autumn Craig

This book is dedicated to all of the victims

that have been exposed to abuse.

May your insecurities vanish,

your self-worth increase and you

feel touched with extra peace and harmony

throughout your journey to your destination

while here on Mother Earth.

-Autumn

Contents

Introduction

If I were to remain silent, I'd be guilty of complicity.

-Albert Einstein

There seems to be a lot less loyalty in this earthly world than I always imagined. Maybe my expectations are too high, or maybe I am not yet where I should be in terms of acceptance of myself or others. I know the Bible commands us not to judge, but I judge constantly, often wondering if this judgment condemns others or just my own soul. I don't judge based on what others possess— their shortcomings, addictions, careers—I judge people based on their attitude and their actions. My mind is an endless flow of thoughts that ask "why?"

Why do people do what they do? Why do people not foresee the outcome of their actions? Why do people not respect the feelings of others? What was someone thinking to have made the decision they did? All of these questions consume my time and my mind. There are days when I think they are the result of the longing I have for a connection with people, and there are days I just chalk it up as my curse.

Chapter One

RITE OF PASSAGE

In troubled families, abuse and neglect

are permitted; It's the talking about them that is forbidden.

-Marcia Sirota

I figured out at a young age that people don't owe you or automatically give you love, nor do they owe you kindness. In a child, that realization leaves deep-seated insecurity that can lead to a lifetime of struggle. I spent part of my childhood feeling like I was in survival mode and not in a world where a home and parents were my security and safe haven. This planted in me the feeling that I have to earn people's love and that love is based on what one deserves. I spent many years of my life thinking that there was no such thing as unconditional, wholehearted love.

Because my parents had divorced, my life had a vacuum that was left for adults with mental disorders to fill. It left my brother and me to have to find a way not only to accept the faults of our own parents, but to adjust to other adults being allowed to hurt us. There were times that I was not sheltered from the pain caused by adults' actions, of which most kids go unaware. I was exposed to them. At times, I was used as a weapon in my parents' battles, and often the battles led to wars. There were many events that instead of turning into a happy memory were tainted with sadness and struggle. It left my mind often wondering if I was responsible for some of the pain.

AND SO IT BEGINS

My parents divorced when I was around nine, and I remember the day as one of the happiest of my childhood. I recall being on the playground at school and my friends consoling me with their heartfelt apologies when I told them my parents were now divorced. While they were trying to make me feel better, I felt guilty for not being sad.

We lived in a modest home when I was growing up in Georgia that mama kept spotlessly clean. It was a three bedroom, one bath small house with wood paneling on the walls and screen doors that led to the country outside. We used a wood stove for heat and had a small gas heater that my older brother, Cory, and I would huddle around on school mornings while waiting for the bus and the wood in the heater to catch fire. My parents owned 12 acres of land that our house and an old wood shed sat on and the land that connected to ours was made up of soybean and wheat fields surrounded by wooded area. If we weren't building forts, making mud pies, or playing in the creeks on the property, we were walking to the country store that was a mile from our house for penny candy.

There were good times when we were together as a family. My father came from a family that consisted of ten other siblings. We usually shared warm summer nights with cousins playing hide and seek and "No Boogers Out Tonight." There were days spent playing softball outside and memories of my parents and their guest playing cards while my cousins and I ran around doing whatever crossed our mind at the time. One thing that I loved and will forever hold dear were the times Daddy played his guitar and sang to us. Two of my favorite songs to hear him play and sing were "Green, Green Grass of Home" and "The Great Speckled Bird." I remember cookouts, days picking grapes for Daddy to make wine, days Mama hooked the screen doors shut so we would not come in until her freshly waxed floors dried as "Harper Valley PTA" blared from the floor stereo. I remember riding bicycles and picking blackberries and during one winter snow Daddy pulling us around behind a tractor on a car hood and making us a fire outside in a tin barrel. Mama made the best snow ice cream and homemade hot cocoa one would ever taste. There were definitely some good times.

But when things went bad, they usually went very bad. Daddy was a no-nonsense kind of man. He was highly intelligent and did not accept one showing self-pity or being what he considered whiney. When he felt we needed correcting, it was usually with a leather belt and after our punishment we were dared to cry. Mama walked on eggshells and so did we at times. There were many nights I laid in bed and listened to my parents fight while Mama cried and begged for it all to stop. It usually ended with Mama being smacked in the face, hit or shoved around. There was never any warning as to what would set Daddy off. One day it was because Cory and I built a tree house and hammered nails in the tree. On a different day it was because Daddy thought I told Mama that he said a curse word. Anything could send him into a rage, and Cory seemed to send him there more than I. One certainty was the whole house caught the brunt of his anger when it happened.

Mama worked second shift, so I would set my alarm clock to wake me up when it was time for her to be home. If I was awake when she got home, then she caught the wrath of Daddy's anger a lot less. One night Cory was away somewhere, and I was home alone with Daddy. He came in my room and told me to get up so we could go find Mama because it was fifteen minutes past the time she should have been getting home from work. As we were leaving the house, Mama was pulling into the driveway. Daddy asked her through gritted teeth where she had been. Mama meekly replied that she was sitting at the store at the end of the road because she was scared to come home. Her explanation led to Daddy hitting her repeatedly and screaming at me to watch as he punished my mama who was a whore. The fight went on for a while and finally ceased with Mama in the floor crying and telling me to make the people and the dog in the corner stop laughing at her. There were no people, nor was there a dog. I picked up the phone to call the police, and Daddy warned me that I would be making a big mistake. He instructed me to call his sister and I obeyed. She came and picked me up late that night and took me to her house. The next day Daddy brought Cory to her house, and that is where we stayed for a while not knowing where our mama was. I found out later that Daddy had taken Mama and admitted her to a psychiatric hospital.

I do not remember the exact time line of all the events after that. I do recall being with one parent while being hidden from the other parent on more than one occasion. There was a lot of anger and hate exchanged between my parents and we were constantly reminded that Daddy was psychotic and Mama was a whore. I had a neighbor who was ten years older than I. On the nights and mornings that I couldn't deal with being at home, I would slip over to her house and hide under the covers in bed with her. She would try to convince me that everything was going to be alright. Details come and go, and there are some that Cory remembers and I don't or vice versa, but I can tell you every detail of the day that it was all supposed to end. The day Mama told me the divorce was final. The day that I thought I would finally get to live what I thought would be a normal life.

Chapter Two

NORMAL IS A DELUSION

A child's innocence is the one gift,

that once stolen, can never be replaced.

-Jaeda DeWalt

In our younger days Cory and I spent a lot of time at my maternal

grandmother's house. She lived close to my cousin, next to a long

red dirt road and a creek. My first cousin, Amy, and I were very

close. She was one year older and we both celebrated our

Birthday's in July. Her mom, Aunt Bet, is my daddy's sister. Amy

and I spent many hot summer days at the creek digging clay out of

the banks, making a playhouse under a bridge, or walking the red

dirt road and doing a lot of daydreaming. I wish that I could have

bottled up one-tenth of our imaginings and conversations. We were

nothing short of sisters, or maybe partners in crime would be a better description. She was one of the best parts of my life and still is to this day.

There were other friends that lived close to Granny, and it was being a part of 'our gang' that taught me the true definition of friendship. We titled each other with secret nicknames, formed private clubs for members only, and our loyalty went even deeper than that. We were blood sisters bonded forever by a simple pinprick. We happily invested our free time in riding dirt bikes, horses and mopeds, fishing or floating the river, and having scavenger hunts in the woods. The days and evenings were filled with adventure only to be replaced with sadness at night when we had to go our separate ways at the end of the red dirt road because it was time to go home. To this day I keep in touch with two of my blood sisters from our gang, and I will always be "Little Sis" to them.

Granny's single wide trailer was always stocked with grits and Carnation milk, lots of Avon products to adorn yourself with, and staying up as late as we wanted. I have great memories of

Granny's house, but as with everything else in my childhood, there was also sadness. Granny lived with a man I called Pawpaw, and he had a strong love for alcohol. A musty, sweaty liquor smell always surrounded him. Some evenings Pawpaw would go from sitting in the living room watching TV to jumping up and running out the door full speed, screaming and flip and roll down a hill in the back yard. I later learned that when he did this he was hallucinating and going through DT's because he was out of alcohol. It was not uncommon to see Pawpaw turn up a bottle of rubbing alcohol and drink it to try to satisfy his addiction when he ran out of liquor. It was not an unusual occurrence for me to sit on a stack of pillows and drive Pawpaw to the local bar and sit next to him and the other drunks for hours. There were no limits to what he exposed me to when I was left in his care.

Not only did he love his alcohol, he loved to touch me inappropriately. I still can't linger to long on the thoughts of this part of my life, though it happened for several years of my childhood. There is no explanation for what sexual abuse does to a child. There is no way to erase the memories and the gut-wrenching feelings that go along with it. I have always wondered if being sexually abused is worse when it happens at the hands of someone you love or someone who is supposed to love and protect you. I can't imagine it not leaving a huge scar regardless, but I do know the shame and memories that do not heal and that you cannot keep from overcoming at times. I know all too well how it devours the innocence in a child's soul and mind and leaves one searching for their value, purpose and worthiness for the rest of their existence. One may think that as the child gets older the memories and pain will lessen. It doesn't work that way. The more you grow and learn about intimacy, the more it haunts you and brings on new emotions that you have to deal with and try to find some type of resolution. Being sexually abused during your childhood leaves damage that doesn't cease when the touching stops, it carries on and stays with you for a lifetime and can often ruin what is supposed to be a sacred bond between and man and a woman.

Another bad habit Pawpaw had when he drank was cursing. He would lay and curse in a drunken state for hours, sometimes days. This compulsion of his led to one of my funniest memories of Granny. One day Amy and I decided to load our red wagon with things we no longer wanted and travel around the neighborhood trying to sell our belongings. Our first stop was Granny's house. We had an old wooden baton with a ball on the end that was covered with glitter. Granny quietly sat and contemplated our merchandise before she purchased the baton. We had no idea why she would want it, but we were thrilled to make a sale. A few days later when I visited Granny again, Pawpaw sat on the couch quietly with a huge purple lump on his forehead. The glittered baton was in the trash can broke in half, and there was no cursing at Granny's house that day.

One evening after enduring hours of one of Pawpaw's cursing spells that didn't seem like it was going to end Granny came to spend the night with us to get away from him. The next morning we went to town grocery shopping, as we did most

Saturday mornings. After we got home, Granny got in her car and drove back to her house. It wasn't long after she left that Mama received a phone call, hurried us to our car and we quickly left for Granny's house. Sitting on the toilet and leaning over onto the sink was a naked dead man with blood coming from his anus and mouth. Pawpaw had died in that position after being on a three-day drunk. I don't know why I was allowed to see him that way before the cops and ambulance got there, but I do remember wondering how a person could swell up like that. Granny was crying and sad, but I was once again overcome with relief. To me it meant that things at Granny's would finally be quieter, a little more peaceful, and maybe even normal.

LIFE CHANGES

Daddy was single for a while after he and Mama divorced. Most nights he could be found sitting in his house in complete darkness. The front door would be open to the night air as he would lounge in his rocking chair drinking Boone's Farm with music playing. He loved the kick-you-in-the-gut type of country music by George Jones and Waylon and the singers from that era. After a few years he remarried, and this was the beginning of his new family that would later include two boys born during their marriage.

Mama remarried shortly after her and Daddy's divorce only for the marriage to end after seven months. She later remarried another man that she met at work and this would add to our childhood saga. The first few months seemed great, but in time our world started unraveling once again.

My new stepdad, Chris, had two children from a previous marriage, and his tolerance for Cory and I quickly grew short. One night my neighbor took me and Cory trick-or-treating. As we were leaving one of the houses after getting our treats, Mama pulled up in a frantic state, ordering us to get in her car. I have no idea how she knew what house to find us at that night, but she did and then she took us to her best friend's house where we stayed the rest of the night. Mama and Chris had got into an argument at work and he became nothing short of irate. The next morning Mama called her father-in-law to go remove Chris from our house. When it was supposed to be safe for us to go home, we pulled up to our house only to be greeted by half of the community along with an ambulance and a few deputy cars. We entered the house to see paramedics strapping my seizing stepdad to a gurney. We soon learned he had overdosed on drugs and after the ambulance took him away, we were left to clean up the evidence of how Chris had spent his night. His truck was hidden in the woods, covered by limbs; all the guns he owned were loaded and placed by the doors and windows, and there were three graves dug in the yard. All the clues left little to the imagination regarding his plans for us that night. My thoughts at the moment the ambulance pulled out of our driveway with him in the back were filled with happiness. I thought that was the end of him being around us. I thought that was the end of the fistfights between him and my brother. I thought that all the ugliness was over. Later my thoughts were proven wrong when I realized that Mama had different thoughts. When he was discharged from the hospital days later, my mother was there to pick him up and bring him home.

I honestly think that when they pulled in the driveway returning home from his hospital stay was the beginning of a secret grudge I would hold against my mother. Things were not the same after he came back home, and I couldn't comprehend how anyone thought they would be. He did what he could to keep Mama happy at first, and Cory and I pretended we cared as we were expected to do. Not only was he back in our house, but he was praised by his family for doing so well after his recovery from his overdose. The man who was on a mission to kill us one night was now receiving all kinds of praise for acting like a normal human being.

I would always get a sick feeling in the pit of my stomach every time I had to be around Chris, which was every day, because he was home at night with us when Mama was at work on second shift. I hated when he came into my bedroom in his underwear and got in bed with me. I hated feeling him touching me. I hated everything about him. One afternoon everything came to the surface again when he and Cory got into a fight. During the drama Mama called from work on her break, and Chris told her that her kids were leaving. Cory had already called Daddy to come get him, and he was begging me to go, too. Cory told me that he could not leave me there alone with our stepdad, and if he had to stay there with me it would be the night that he killed Chris. I told him I would go to Daddy's for the night, but Mama would straighten everything out the next day, and then I was going to come back home. Daddy came to get us, which led to a fight between him and Chris, who then pulled a gun on Daddy. Mama left work early after her disturbing phone call home only to pull up as we were getting in the car to leave with Daddy. We drove away as my mother was standing next to Chris, who was still holding a pistol, stood in the yard and watched.

The next morning Daddy and my stepmother took me and Cory to a lawyer's office where we were asked about the events of the previous day, some papers were signed, and then we were dropped off at school to finish our day. During lunch one of my friends that rode the same school bus as I asked me if we were moving. I didn't really understand why she was asking, so I responded that we just spent the night at Daddy's house and would be going home that afternoon. She said that as the bus went by our house that morning, people were loading stuff on a truck, and it looked like we were moving. I called home after school that day and no one answered my phone call, nor did anyone answer for the next three days.

My graduation from eighth grade was on the evening of the third day of being at Daddy's house. Mama was not at my graduation, which seemed to confirm my belief that she had left us to be with Chris. After graduation ended, my stepmother told me she had somewhere to take me. We pulled into the local hospital and walked into a room where Mama laid in a hospital bed with white cream all over her face and forehead to cover burns on her skin. After we left with Daddy three nights earlier, Mama told Chris that he had to leave. They spent the night arguing, and the next morning he left after throwing gas from a plastic jug on her as she lay on the couch. He then tossed a match on her and set her on fire.

Mama was later discharged from that hospital and taken to a place in Tennessee to heal, gather her mind, and prepare to get her life back together. She was gone for most of the summer, and Cory and I remained at Daddy's. During that time Daddy took us home to clean the house, and the scene within those walls will forever be burned in my mind, just as the footprints were burned into the living room floor. Yellowish dust from the fire extinguisher covered the walls and furniture, and the couch had a large burned area. I don't know how I was supposed to process the scene before me that day and the images that it left in my mind. Once again I didn't understand how such a horrific outcome had brought me a little peace, but I do remember that I felt a small amount of happiness that day because Daddy was doing something nice for Mama.

Mama came home after her time away, and Cory and I moved back home to be with her. To say the least, it was stressful for the first few months. Chris would still cut screens on our windows, make threats, or just appear out of nowhere wherever we happened to be. Finally one day it all ended. I don't know why or how, but it did. After that, Mama was the happiest I can remember her ever being in my childhood. She would take trips with her friends and attend concerts and events. We would spend time riding around while we listened to music, dancing, or talking for hours. I remember Mama laughing a lot during this time, which was something new to experience, and I think she was truly for once happy.

A few years later, Mama remarried to a man who did not have one ounce of meanness in him. His wife had passed away and he had a son the same age as Cory. We call him Papa because that's what my brother's children named him after they were born.

When I refer to my parents, I am referring to him and Mama. It was after they married that life was finally what I called normal for a while. I lived with them until the middle of my senior year and then, because I could not agree with anything Mama said to me, I moved out to live with an aunt.

Mama always blamed our differences on me and chalked it up to me acting out. I am sure it was mostly my fault. I was at a point in my life that I started trying to put things together and really questioning the past. I didn't think either of my parents cared about me, and I didn't feel they had any right to give me advice on what was a good decision or a bad decision. Their recommendations on how I should live my life were not graciously received, nor appreciated. I worked after school and on weekends to pay for my car and insurance and to buy the things I needed. The night of my high school graduation I had spent the entire day wondering if either of my parents would be there. They both were. Neither spoke to me, but they both attended, which was more than I had ever gotten before.

Chapter Three

MISUNDERSTOOD

Run my dear, from anything that may not strengthen

your precious budding wings. Run like hell my dear,

from anyone likely to put a sharp knife into the sacred,

tender vision of your beautiful heart.

-Hafiz

The older I got, the more I came to realize that not only do we inherit the consequences of our parents' mistakes, but we also create our own adversity. I intended for high school to be my time to shine. I finally built up enough nerve to speak to people, and some even considered me funny. I felt I had a little control over my destiny and was not just linked to the turmoil others had brought into my life. I was smart enough to be in college prep classes, and I had made some very close friends. I befriended a girl in eighth grade, Kristi, who became my best friend through the remainder of our school years and then some. She would change my life and give me the confidence to live. She didn't care about my home situation or what my circumstances were. She was popular, smart, a cheerleader, and had the fairy-tale life I longed for. The most unbelievable thing about her was she wanted me to be a part of her life and included me in everything she did. We were constantly laughing. Even when we sat and cried together over one of our misfortunes, we would always end up laughing. Kristi and I would skip school, sneak out after curfew, lie in bed at night and made animal noises to the top of our lungs, double-date, attend parties, and took a few trips together. But the best thing about us was that we were each other's best friend. She didn't judge. She didn't need to know why. She didn't need anyone to accept her. Kristi loved life, and she loved me.

Throughout my high school years I had my share of loves and plenty of dates. I had the bad boy who was my first major crush. We spent days riding horses and swimming in nearby creeks and lakes. I had the popular guy who would write notes to me on my hand in French class. I fell in love with a football player who would stick by me and be my on-again, off-again high school boyfriend until I graduated. I dated the rich basketball player who bought me gifts and gave me the excitement of shopping and spending time in his family's beautiful homes and nice cars. I built a solid friendship with a smart guy from an upper-class family who tried from our days in eighth grade until we graduated to be my boyfriend. I always dismissed his offer because inside I felt I wasn't good enough for him. I had the sweetest guy who lived close to me, whom I traveled many back roads with listening to music, spent evenings playing video games, and he took me to my very first concert. And I still had my gang that I had grown up with. With my circle of girlfriends I had beach trips and trips to Savannah for St. Patrick's Day, days lying out at the lake, nights camping, and parties at my home when my mother was out of town. I had the cute, funny guy, Michael, who is still to this day one of my best friends. After Michael and I left our dates on the weekends and went home to make curfew, we would then sneak out together to ride back roads, break into the local college gym

and sit in the sauna, or lie on the bank at the lake and talk about

everything and anything that came to mind.

I had all of these experiences and memories to take with me

after high school, though at the time they were shadowed with a

layer of "I don't deserve this" and thoughts of "if people only

knew." It was not until I was older that I realized that I was the

only person who held me back. Some people labeled me as a bit

snobbish, when in reality I was shy or didn't have the nerve to

speak for fear of rejection. Some people saw me as pretty, when

inside I always felt like I didn't measure up. I wish that I had

learned a long time ago that there is a difference between

embracing life and trying to make it a fairy tale. I wish that I'd had

realized that my circumstances didn't define me. I wish that I'd

had someone to explain all of that to me. I wish I had someone tell

me when I didn't make the cheerleading squad that it wasn't

because I wasn't good enough, but because the week of tryouts I

could only make it to two practices because I didn't have a ride home. I wish that when I failed a geometry test someone had told me that it was normal because geometry was hard and it just meant that I needed to study more or ask for a tutor. I wish when I was dumped by a guy someone had told me that it was because that is what guys do, not because I wasn't worthy. But I didn't. I took all the normal hardships in life and added them to the pile of not-so-normal hardships that I had experienced and combined it all to reach the conclusion that I was totally screwed up and unworthy. I wasn't aware that there are different levels of failure and that everyone shares some of the struggles I had experienced.

AIR FORCE DAYS, AIR FORCE WAYS

There are moments in life that are disregarded by some people but turn out to be life changing for others. I had one of these moments soon after beginning my senior year in high school. Everyone was in the cafeteria after taking placement exams, and my friends were discussing college plans. They were sharing who would be roommates, what careers they had chosen, and what colleges had accepted them. I sat at the lunchroom table frozen and thinking. I realized that I had never held a serious conversation with my parents regarding college, I had never been advised regarding the need to fill out college applications, and I didn't have the financial means to go to college. I had said through my years growing up that I wanted to be a lawyer, an air traffic controller, a model, a nurse, a journalist, and many other things that had intrigued me, but never had I prepared or had anyone to give me guidance or explain to me the steps it took to prepare for college. I took the college prep classes, I fulfilled my requirement of two years of foreign language, I struggled to pass history, and I took the SAT test. But I never put it all together and figured out a plan from making it all work.

So there I sat with another failure to add to my list. My friends were doing what normal teenagers do, and I had no idea where I was going to go from there. I stood up from the table to make my way to the bathroom so I could isolate myself because, once again, I didn't fit in or have anything to contribute to the conversation. On my way out of the cafeteria, I saw the answer for my future sitting in the hallway. I picked up a few brochures from a table, went home at the end of the day, and pondered my options. The next day I called and made an appointment that would change the course of my life. Now at lunch I could join in on the conversation about future dreams because I now had a plan. But, most importantly, I had an answer when someone asked me what I was going to do after graduation. I could proudly reply that I was going to basic training because I was joining the United States Air Force. That wiped away all my poor planning and all of the guidance that I was never offered. That wiped away having to find money for college, my ignorance of not being aware that I had to apply for colleges, and having to figure out where was I going to go when everyone else was living in the dorms or renting an apartment while attending college. Joining the military answered all of the questions that I had no answer to before and then some.

After graduation came the last carefree summer I would spend in Georgia, waiting until my time to leave for basic training. I moved back in with Mama and Papa for the summer. When the day came to leave, three of my friends came to my house, picked me up, and drove me to the airport. Mama was too distraught to take me. I remember the long goodbyes, and the look frozen on the face of my on-again, off-again boyfriend when he realized we really weren't going to get married. I soaked in the amazing feeling of thinking that I was out of there. I was responsible for myself and I could leave all the memories and shame that I had carried behind. I was starting my life on my own terms and going to a place where no one knew anything about me and the ground for all of us would be level. We would all be the same. I was free. I thought I was free, anyway.

I had no idea of one thing about the military. I had no clue what stand at attention meant. I had no knowledge of anything that had to do with the Department of Defense. I soon learned, and I learned quickly the hard way. Basic training could be described as anything except being free. Looking back, I can tell you two decisions that I was free to make for myself. One was to try to go unnoticed, and the other was to say "ma'am" or "sir" as many times as possible in one sentence. Those were the only two things related to having freedom that I can remember. But I loved it. I loved the unity, the dedication, the challenge, the purpose, and the fact that we were all in the same situation and we were all surviving together. I loved everyone cheering each other on during obstacle courses, trying to encourage each other to finish the run, rushing out of bed at reveille before the sun was up to line up on the drill pad, braiding hair at night before bed, praying with each other in the dark, and the quietness that surrounded us after lights out even though there were thirty girls sleeping in one bay. I loved the one for all and all for one attitude. I loved the idea of no comrade left behind, the feeling that we were all going to make sure that we all made it. I loved the smirk of pride on the training instructor's face when we beat our brother flight in a competition, or when we pulled off a detail that the training instructor was sure we would fail at. I loved that we were a combination of different colors, religions, and nationalities but we all shared the same purpose. I remember turning around at chapel on Thanksgiving Day when my training instructor summoned me and seeing Mama and Papa standing behind the back pew. They had flown in to surprise me and spend a few hours with me for Thanksgiving. I remember thinking that they were now on my turf and in my world, and I felt proud of what they were looking at. I also remember that almost the first words out of Mama's mouth that day were "You finally learned to stand up straight and stop slouching."

When I was signing in to the military, I took a test and scored well enough to be guaranteed a language interpreter job. Accepting the position meant I had to obligate myself to at least six years of service for my first enlistment. I opted to decline that position and signed up for four years instead. The recruiter advised me that they couldn't guarantee me another position since I declined the language interpreter position, so I would be assigned to a job that the military felt they needed me in. This could have been anything from a cook to a bus driver. I did not realize the importance of a language interpreter position or how differently that would have impacted my life and my military career. It was a position that was well respected in the service. I also did not realize that it was not easy to score high on the D Lab test and you were considered rather smart if you did. That explained why the army, marine, and navy recruiters all congratulated me as we were waiting for our test scores the day we took them. That is just one more thing that I would greatly have appreciated someone taking the time to explain to me. After declining the language interpreter position, I was assigned to logistics and would do on-the-job training at my first duty assignment.

After basic training and before I reported to my first duty assignment, I flew home. My friends picked me up at the airport so I could surprise Mama with a visit. I walked in the house as Mama was digging out a pair of boots my friend said she was there to borrow. When Mama turned around and saw me, she knocked me to the floor with excitement and hugs. I felt like a whole different kind of grown up that day. I can't tell you anything else I recall about that week at home except for my on-again, off-again high school boyfriend sitting on my bed as I unpacked, holding my dog tags and staring at them with tears in his eyes. I can remember that moment clearly and thinking, we are so different and I am not good enough for you. And then my next memory is of packing my car with everything I could fit into it. Michael, my best guy friend from high school, drove his truck in front of me with his flashers on escorting me to the interstate. At the exit I was to get on the interstate, I gave Michael a hug bye, bought a pack of Vantage menthols and smoked the entire six-hour drive to North Carolina in my Air Force blues with the radio blasting. I arrived at base, stayed in the base motel because I arrived a few days too early and my dorm room wasn't ready. I spent my first three days of work at the wrong building with the wrong squadron, and was finally picked up and escorted to my correct duty station to be greeted by my female sergeant with the words "Where have you been" and "You look like a pixie."

REBIRTHING YOUR SOUL WITHOUT

INSTRUCTIONS

Growing up in Georgia you inherit a warm southern night feeling

that is really hard to explain. I always thought this feeling could

not be topped. That was until I had to adjust to North Carolina's

southern night feeling, and to say the least, it is not describable.

Georgia nights leave you in a sea of humidity, but North Carolina

nights had a sense of sweetness to their stickiness. It would take

an entire series of books to write about my Air Force days, but to

sum it up, I spent the first few months testing the waters with the

newfound freedom of living my own life. Just the feeling I had as I

drove through the gates to the base for the first time was enough

for me to smile about and revel in for months. I was free to be

myself without any restrictions or anyone to please. I was for the

first time in my life able to do what I wanted to do and be who I

wanted to be. I didn't have to cater to anyone for fear of upsetting

them, namely my parents.

After a few weeks on base, I developed a friendship with two girls. Sandy was from New York, Catholic, and a ball of energy. She had brown hair and the most amazing smile. Dece was a girl of color, always laughing and making jokes, and she carried herself with ease and calmness. I was raised in a white community in a country setting and my family was Southern Baptist. I did not realize my ignorance of being prejudice until I left home. Their friendship made me realize that labels are an injustice and a burden to carry around. These two friends would stick by me until my enlistment in the service was over and beyond.

I also befriended a guy from Virginia I nicknamed Townie. He was shy and had a way of dealing with me using sensitivity and calmness. Townie introduced me to raising windows during a rain storm, incense, and the sweet sound of Enigma. He also taught me that no matter where you come from or how damaged you may feel, you are still special. He is the first person who actually introduced me to what peace felt like. I befriended another guy from California, Matt, who introduced me to batting cages and Baskin-Robbins and helped me discover my love for Aerosmith. He taught me that a man and a woman can really love each other and not have a sexual relationship. He held my hand, cuddled with me when I was lonely, and had my back when the world crashed around me because of my own actions. He loved me when I was wild and single, and he loved me the same after I was married and had a child. We created a circle of friends who still keep in touch and share memories that no one could replace and time cannot steal away. We were young, and all of us were finding out what and who we were on the inside while learning and depending on each other.

My friends and I spent nights as a group at the local bar called Pirates outside the back gate of the base. We would circle around the dance floor singing "Bye-bye, Miss American Pie" at the top of our lungs. We had nights sleeping on Wrightsville Beach with our blankets and coolers, days lying out by the base pool, evenings playing volleyball or softball or working out in the gym.

There were more nights shared than I can count huddled around the pool table in the day room funneling beer and cracking jokes on each other. Sandy and I spent weekends traveling to New York or to Georgia to visit our families, days perming or coloring hair and doing nails, watching movies all day in our pajamas, and mornings that she woke me up with hot cocoa because she knew how bad I hated getting up. Dece and I spent days at work laughing at the madness and each other, burping contests to see who had to buy the next round of beer, moments mopping floors and doing details together because we couldn't keep our mouth shut to our superiors or we had disrespected authority. And there were so many other people that impacted my life and brought me happiness. People who will never know what they meant to me, and I will probably never have the opportunity to tell them because I will never see them again.

From everyone that I surrounded myself with I learned something or they brought me a moment's peace. My sergeants taught me that someone can chew your butt for something and still have your back the next minute. My friends taught me that people can be total opposites and come from all different walks of life and still love one another. And there was my very first supervisor that called me a pixie the first day she met me who took on the role as my second mother and went to extremes to take care of me and still does to this very day.

MY VERY OWN LOVE AND WAR STORY

Loving you was like going to war; I never came back the same.

-Warsan Shire

After a few short lived relationships, I found myself intrigued with a military cop of Italian decent. He was the first person I saw the very first day I entered the Air Force base. He was working the entrance gate to the base and he was amazingly beautiful. We chatted for a few minutes as I was trying to figure out how to get on base and where I needed to go after entering. He would later try to talk to me on several different occasions, but I would always dismiss our flirtations as anything other than just that. My hesitations about him came from the girl talk at the dorms I resided in about how irresistibly dangerous he was and how he would not commit to one girl. The same girls who talked about him were also the ones who would melt any time he came in sight.

A year after being at base as I was entering the gate for the fourth or fifth time that particular day, he finally stopped me and asked if he could help me. I informed him that I didn't need any help and I felt compelled to follow up his offer by telling him that I had heard he was a dog. He assured me through his smile that he wasn't a dog and he charmed me enough during that conversation that I drove away only after giving him my phone number. The following Saturday morning I was awakened by my phone ringing and he was on the other end of the line requesting for me to get up and get ready to spend the day with him. For our first date he took me on a short trip to the Outer Banks of North Carolina. It consisted of a breezy day lying on the beach, talking and trying to figure one another's personalities out. I have to admit that it could not have been a more perfect date. I do not remember all of the topics of our conversations that day, but I do remember one thing he said that calmed a few of my insecurities: "You are prettier than any other girl on this beach." That sentence from the beautiful-skinned forbidden Italian guy will never leave my mind. Nor will the ride home in his Rocky with the top down as I snuggled inside

of his sweatshirt. From that day forward it was just us. We didn't

need to discuss our status with each other or declare we were a

couple. We just knew that we were meant to be together and we

could not have been any happier. Our connection just was and

needed no explanation nor do I think we could have found one.

We needed no one else and spent every minute we could

alone with each other sharing evenings and nights. When he spoke

and interacted with anyone else it was with confidence, but when

he spoke and interacted with me it was with nothing but softness.

He was the guy that opened doors, carried bags, and held my coat

for me as I put it on. He was the guy that heated up the vehicle on

cold days so it would be warm when he opened the door for me to

get in after a piggy back ride thru the parking lot. He was the one

that would shine my boots and iron my military uniforms. He

didn't try to have sex with me at first like the other girls said he

would do. He was patient and waited for the intimate moments to

happen giving no pressure for it to be sooner than I wanted.

After a few months of dating we drove to New Jersey to spend a weekend with his family. During our trip, we visited the Boardwalk at the beach near his home one evening and rode some of the carnival rides. It was then that I realized I had been nauseated on and off during the trip. Upon returning to base from our weekend away, the nausea had subsided and it was dismissed from my mind. One weekend soon after our return from New Jersey, we went to a manmade lake near the base and spent the day swimming and diving off of a cliff. A few days later while I was at work, I became very nauseated and started having painful stomach cramps. I went to my dorm room to lie down, only to later call my supervisor. She came and picked me up and drove me to the hospital. A few hours later after lab work had been completed and an exam was done, I sat in the waiting room and listened as the sound of his cleats came down the hall way. He was playing in a softball game and someone told him that I was at the hospital. I had to look at his soft brown eyes and tell him I was having a miscarriage. He never faltered. He took me back to his dorm room, spread out a towel on his bed, and I spent that night in his room with him holding me and asking me every five minutes if I was I alright. He kept repeating the words "this changed nothing."

We went to Georgia the following weekend to face my parents, and I sat in silence and watched as he never one time stumbled while answering their questions and explaining what had happened. He was so sure of everything, and he dealt with it all while I sat there confused and ashamed. His responses were so calm and left no room for any doubt when he answered that he loved me and would marry me. This guy that every girl swooned over sat and talked about how he loved me. He protected me and dealt with all the hard stuff so that I did not have to. I asked him many times why. His reply was always, "You respected yourself and that made me respect you. You were different than all the other girls."

It was less than a month after the miscarriage that I sat in a parking lot late one night crying as it seemed my world was falling apart. I had to tell him bye as he boarded a bus because he had been called for a deployment to Cuba. I remember feeling so abandoned. I had to face all my emotions and confusion alone. I was also left to face the rest of the base without my best friend and protection. I felt like I was left with so many broken pieces scattered around me that I needed to completely sweep everything away and start over. I fell into a realm of confusion that overtook my logic. I waited until one of his phone calls from Cuba to end our relationship by phone, even though he assured me that it was not over until he returned and I told him in person.

I spent the next few months redirecting myself and trying to find some conciliation for what had happened. Looking back now, I am sure it was hormones that overtook me. I visited the Base Chaplin to try to get some understanding and forgiveness for what I had done. I started hanging out with my old friends, again. And I tried to pretend the miscarriage never happened. It was a couple of months later that I was deployed to Saudi Arabia and I would not be at the base when the beautiful Italian cop returned from his deployment. I had received a few more months that I didn't have to face him and own up to the guilt I felt for cliff diving, which I was positive was the cause of the miscarriage. I could not come to terms with how I was so reckless and did not make sure that I was not pregnant after having nausea and before I spent that day at the lake. I could not accept that my actions caused us to lose something that would have forever changed our lives.

BEING CALLED TO DUTY

There is something to be said about living on a military base, but there are really no words to describe it. A strong feeling of safety and closeness develops among brothers and sisters in arms. People seem to form a certain impression of what being in the military must be like, but in reality I feel it is completely the opposite of what people who have not served think. My time in the military was one of the most carefree times of my life. I would lie in bed at night and listen to planes take off and land on the flight line near my dorm. I spent many days driving around the flight line with my sunroof open to see the jets coming over my car to land a few hundred feet away. Pope Air Force Base was home to F-16 fighter jets, A-10 Thunderbolt II attack jets, and C-130 cargo planes that carried the elite 82nd Airborne from Fort Bragg to their deployment missions. I lived on one side of the flight line and I worked on the other side. There was almost always something going on to keep you busy and entertained, and when there wasn't, you welcomed the calm moments when you could rest and prepare for the next round of excitement.

With all of the happiness I found in the military came also probably the worst feelings I would experience. On March 23, 1994, an F-16 and a C-130 collided in the air, resulting in the F-16 crashing into a C-141 at the end of the runway on Green Ramp. The 82nd Airborne troops were loading on to the C-141 to go up for a parachute jump. The explosion and the smell that day is something I will never forget. The final death toll was twenty-four paratroopers killed on our own soil before us during a simple training exercise. No one knew what to say or do for days as the crash and recovery efforts went on. In the coming days after the accident we would all stand in silence as the churches in the city rang their bells at the same time. I don't know if I have ever experienced a worse case of the cold chills that overtook my body.

A few months after that accident I found myself standing at attention on the flight line on September 20, 1994, as the Air Force Two landed and Vice President Al Gore commended the Joint

Task Force for its efforts in Operation Uphold Democracy. A month after that, on October 8, 1994, at 0530 hours, I received a call from my sergeant and through the phone she boldly stated the word "Recall." It happened to be on a morning after a night out with my friends and half of them were still asleep in my dorm room. Recall meant that I had twenty minutes to report to work, and something was probably not going to be good. We reported to our duty stations and were then met with the word "deployment." Iraqi soldiers were lining up at the border during the Desert Shield–Desert Storm era, and we were being summoned to deploy.

Twenty-four hours later vaccinations had been received, my will had been made, and my power of attorney paperwork signed. I loaded on a C-130 with twenty-eight men I had never seen before to fly to Saudi Arabia. I sat on the plane for five hours as it hummed and vibrated its way through the air before I finally spoke to anyone on the plane. A guy sitting next to me on the nets that were our seats finally looked at me and said, "You are going to have to talk to us sometime." I concluded he was right so I informed him that I needed to use the restroom. After the other guys laughed for a bit, they held up a plastic curtain for me to urinate in a bucket on the bouncing plane. It was at that point that I felt it confirmed that we had bonded. Five days we spent on an airplane flying with a fleet of fifteen planes. We stopped in different countries along the way, including Portugal and Italy, to refuel and maintenance the planes. Although I had just met them, the guys I was flying over with took care of me as if they were my brothers. I never felt nervous or scared except during the landing in the desert of Saudi Arabia in the middle of the night. I was excited, ready, and amazed at what loyalty in a group of people can create and overcome.

After arriving in Saudi and processing in, I met up with many of my friends from home base who had arrived in Saudi a few days prior to me since they made the trip in jets rather than a prop plane. We did our tour and made our memories in a foreign land. We worked long days and nights, played volleyball every chance we got, held out through sandstorms together, and worked with soldiers from other countries who were there for the same reason we were. At a time that was supposed to be one of the scariest times of our life, there was a magical feeling in being there. Everyone was united, and we found any reason possible to laugh and joke and be there for one another.

I met up with a guy from home base while I was over there, and we started spending time together. After our deployment, I returned to Pope AFB and my Italian cop was there to greet me and make me tell him to his face that it was over. A few weeks after that, I went to his dorm room one night to talk to him, and another girl was in his room. I never knocked on his door. I left and I moved on with my life. I soon after married the guy that I spent time with in Saudi.

A year and one month after being married, we welcomed a baby girl to the world. A few months after she was born, I had to take her to Georgia and leave her while we prepared the base for Hurricane Fran to hit and then clean up the aftermath that was left behind. That taught me that that I did not want to raise my daughter in an environment that I may have to leave her at any given time. So after my four-year enlistment in the service was up, I packed up a U-Haul with my jeep in tow, strapped my six-month-old baby girl in her car seat on the passenger side, and moved back to Georgia. My husband still had time left on his enlistment, so he stayed behind. I drove home to Georgia that day feeling as lost as I did the day I left Georgia when I was eighteen. I was returning to the place I had spent so many years trying to leave behind, and I was bringing back a precious little child with me.

Chapter Four

FINDING WHERE YOUR SOUL BELONGS

Boundaries are a part of self-care.

They are healthy, normal, and necessary.

-Doreen Virtue

I spent my first few months back in the civilian world trying to obtain a job, settling into our new home, being very alone because my husband was still in the military, and realizing that I did not belong where I was. I had left and created a whole new world, only to leave it and return to where I had started from. Kristi and I picked up where we left off and spent a lot of time together. After we got our kids to sleep, we would stay up all night every chance we got talking and laughing. I wasn't sure if my husband was coming to Georgia when his enlistment was up or if he even had the desire to. I started working, being a mom, and dealing with that feeling inside. That awkward, I don't belong feeling that churned inside of me. My husband did eventually move to Georgia to be with us, only for us to struggle with our marriage. Two years after we were married, we called it quits. Or I called it quits and he agreed. There was no abuse, there was no hate, there was nothing that I can pinpoint and say that is why we divorced. It just didn't work. Looking back now, I am sure it is because neither of us cared if it worked. It is sad to say, but true. We both made our share of mistakes, we both contributed to the failure, we both were to blame, but neither of us hated each other for it. I honestly think we just had no idea where to go with our marriage, so we let it dissolve. But out of the marriage we had a beautiful baby girl that I had failed just like my parents had failed me. She would be raised in a divided family.

Along with filing for a divorce, I quit my full-time job, started a part-time job at the 9-1-1 call center as an operator, and I started nursing school full time. It was during this time that I lost my best friend since eighth grade. Kristi died in a car wreck, and I was the last person to see her and talk to her that day. We left her workplace after she helped me pick out a dress there, and I was following her to her house to pick up her children and go out for dinner. I took a different route at the end of the trip to her home. I made it to her house, but she never did. Kristi had a wreck not far from her home. I took her two children to my house and spent the night trying to console a two year old boy and a seven month old little girl who were crying and missing their mother. The next morning Kristi's older sister called and requested that I to come to the hospital. We sat with Kristi and held her hands as they turned off the life support machine.

I not only lost my best friend, I lost a chunk of my heart. I lost the person who was there for me when my marriage was falling apart and she let me know that I would survive. I lost the girl who, when I was alone and felt like I was drowning in my own thoughts and mistakes, let me know there would still be tomorrow. I lost the girl who told me I was weird and had always been weird, but it only made her love me more. I lost the girl who, when I was tripping and felt like everything around me was dissolving, could burst out in a hymn or song to the top of her lungs and let me know that things don't always have to be dramatic or serious. I lost the only person who had loved me consistently for years and had accepted everything about me and my family and had probably been the only bit of sanity I had for a major part of my life. I lost someone I was so proud to call my friend.

LEARNING WHAT YOU ARE MADE OF

I finished school and received my LPN certification, began taking classes working toward an RN license, and started a new job at a local physician's office. It was through that job that I bonded with four of the most amazing ladies, who became a part of my life in the best way. Brenda was the mother of a friend of mine from High School and she taught me so much about life without even knowing. She had a laid back attitude and an explanation of "everything doesn't have to make sense" that brought me calmness. She showed me that it was acceptable to figure things out as you go. Debbie had a funny sense of humor and was my go to for jokes or deep conversations. She always offered the kindest smile when you looked at her. Rena was the sweetest, most accepting person I had ever met and to this day is a huge part of my heart and life. She taught me the gift of being able to accept others and let things just be. I became friends with a girl in another town, Jennifer, whom I love and I am grateful for to this day. She filled up some of my loneliness by loving my daughter and I as if she had been a part of our life forever. We would go four-wheeling, travel to other towns for concerts, or just hang out and drink sweet tea and enjoy our conversations. She introduced me to her group of friends who soon came to be my group of friends, also. Each of these ladies added to my life and taught me qualities that I wanted to possess.

The next six years of my life after my divorce were spent dating, being a mom, and trying to figure out where I belonged. I made mistakes, but as I look back, this was one of the most beautiful times of my life mentally. I figured out that spending time with my daughter was worth more than a million nights out on the town. I was able to focus on making a home of happiness for me and my daughter. We raised animals, planted gardens, painted nails, became members of a nearby church, had picnics, went on adventures, and spent many afternoons walking trails and dirt roads.

It was during this time in my life that I realized that I could be very ghastly on the inside, also. I saw that I could be very selfish. I became aware that I could be very strong, yet I was never far from being weak. I began to understand that a lot of the not belonging that I felt inside came from the shame of mistakes I had made. I realized that when I want to hurt someone, I can cut to the core and I show no mercy. But only when you recognize the bad in yourself, you can start to grow and become something different and better. And I spent my time focusing on growing and accepting change and trying to become the woman and mother that I deemed acceptable in my mind's definition. I had only myself to depend on, and I knew that I had to be strong enough for me and my child and I would not let us fail.

People say that you have to learn how to be alone before you can be content with someone. I conquered this feat. I spent sleepless, lonely nights wondering and searching for things that I did not know if they would ever come to be. I spent weekends that I hated to see the evening come at the end of the day because I knew a restless night would follow. I spent nights crying myself to sleep because I longed to feel someone's touch. I spent days wondering if I would ever share a home with someone again. But in all of the time alone, I learned there can also be peace. I made decisions without the guidance of anyone else. I had only myself to rely on to pay bills and put food on the table. I was a twentysomething year old woman, and I had my own place to live, my own car, and my own beautiful blonde and curly headed little girl. I didn't have to settle in the future, because I knew that alone I could make it. That is a wonderful feeling and one that can only be felt and fully appreciated when dutifully earned.

GIVING OTHER PEOPLE POWER OVER YOU

After six years of being a single mother, I met a guy from Tennessee. He was different. He was full of happiness and kindness. He didn't try to control me or have insecurities I needed to feed into. He was everything that I wanted and felt would make my life complete. We dated by rotating weekends that we would visit the other and after a few months he asked me to marry him. I said yes after he agreed upon three wishes I wanted. I wanted to have another child that I could raise with a husband because that was something that I had always strongly desired. I also requested that we did not move to Tennessee and the third wish was that when the children were grown, we would move to live close to some form of water. He had a vasectomy in his previous marriage, so he went to the urologist before we married to make sure he could have it reversed. Our answer was yes and if he did it within the next two years, the chances of us having a child were pretty remarkable. He agreed with my wishes and we would soon be married.

Our first two years of marriage were spent living in my home in Georgia. Two weekends out of the month we would travel to Tennessee to see his two children who lived with their mother. My husband had married his high school sweetheart after their high school graduation when she told him she was pregnant. They had a son and he then adopted her daughter that she had from a previous relationship and took her as his own. His daughter and I never really formed a good relationship. I wasn't her mother (which I did not want to be) and she wasn't going to allow me to perform the role of being her stepmother. I did form a bond with his son, John, and would later spend many nights trying to console him over the phone when he was sad and wanted a different life than he was living. After many discussions with John about his unhappiness, we filed for and received custody of him. My husband moved to Tennessee to finish raising him and find a home for what would be our new combined family. During this time I stayed in Georgia and waited until he found a place for us to live.

The time apart caused hardship in our marriage and created some distance between us.

My husband was in Tennessee four months before my daughter and I moved there to join him and John. It was a hard adjustment for all of us, involving many mixed emotions, tangled between my wanting to be there and feeling I should have never moved my child to a new place. My daughter was very sad the first few months and had a hard time adjusting to say the least. I would come home from work to chalk written messages on the driveway stating how bad she hated Tennessee. I received phone calls from her school daily with her crying on the other end of the line begging me to come get her. Combining families was rather hard and emotional to say the least. It definitely was not something that I had prepared myself or my child well enough for.

On top of dealing with my new home and my daughter's sadness, we were trying to combine our new family and the changes caused sacrifices for everyone involved. The changes led to a difficult relationship once again between me and my husband.

After a couple of times of packing up my stuff and my daughter and driving back and forth between Georgia and Tennessee, my daughter and I finally stayed in Tennessee and worked harder at making it our home.

Things finally settled and everyone adjusted to our now happy combined family. My daughter made new friends at school and became involved in cheerleading and basketball. John seemed to like living with us and we spent many nights sitting and talking and became very close. He and I made up a name for our family because it seemed to be so different than other families. We called ourselves the "Googlehiemers." I felt things were stable enough that I began wanting to try to have a baby. My husband avoided getting his vasectomy reversed by always saying we would discuss it later or it wasn't the time.

Two years after we were in Tennessee, when John was fourteen, things in our home started changing again. John became distant from us and seemed to be establishing a better relationship with his mother. Our happy home turned into a home of constant conflict once again. I wasn't allowed to say anything to upset John

because when I did his mother would call my husband and tell him

how horrible I was and how it was not my place to try to parent her

child. My husband's solution was for me to not say anything so

there would be a need for them to be upset. This caused me a lot of

mixed emotions and the thought that my feelings didn't matter. I

worked to contribute financially to our family, carried medical

insurance on all of us, and paid for all of John's things, but I was

not allowed to have any say so over how my home was ran.

It was during this time that my husband and I came to find

out that John was not my husband's biological son. John's sister

had told several people in town that he had a different biological

father. John had made some remarks that led us to wonder if he,

also, had heard what was being said. My husband and I secretly did

a DNA test to put an end to the rumors, but the results were not in

our favor. The DNA test determined that John wasn't my

husband's biological son. After several emotional nights of

discussing it, we decided not to tell John or anyone else. We loved

John, and my husband didn't care whose blood he carried; he had raised John and wanted to continue to do so.

A few months after the DNA test, John's mother decided to file to regain custody of him. After she filed the paperwork and during an argument between her and my husband one night, my husband told her about the DNA test. She pleaded for my husband not to tell John. My husband hoped that the secret would shame the mother enough to stop trying to get custody of him and let us finish raising him. It turned out differently. After another argument with the mother a week or so later, she immediately hung up the phone and told John the big secret. The next day she filed for a court-ordered paternity test and she established paternity with John's biological father. She did her best to destroy the relationship between John and my husband. Her methods worked and with her encouragement, John chose to not be a part of our lives. All the drama reached a point that led to a day of my husband standing in front of a judge saying that he still wanted to raise John. The judge's heartbreaking response was that he did not have that right any longer as a parent. It was up to the mother and John whether my husband could continue to have a part in John's life. John testified that he didn't want to see my husband at that time as the mother sat and smiled in the courtroom. My husband had also lost his relationship with his adopted daughter a few years prior to this. She had chosen not to be a part of our lives because of the same mother's influence. She was spending time with her biological father and did not want to see us because we would not tolerate her choices and wanted her to make better decisions. That led to her mother convincing her that we didn't love her and she didn't have to see us. Their opinion seemed to be that nothing was needed from us except money for child support and medical bills. They especially did not want our opinions or guidance.

All of this was not as simple as it looks on paper. It was seven years of pure hell, sleepless nights, court cases that ended up in Supreme Court, marriage and family counseling sessions, so many mistakes made by each and every one of us, and in the end a lot of broken mangled hearts. I was arrested during the process based on lies from my husband's ex-wife. She worked at the same hospital as I and took a copy of the warrant for my arrest to human resources in hopes of getting me fired. I spent days passing her in the hallway as she and her best friend made snide remarks and smirks. I did not lose my job, but I did have to go to court and suffer through the embarrassment of the situation, which ended well. I also had to live with my husband who always responded with a simple reply of ignore it each time something bad happened. Every time that he said it, I felt a little less vindicated and a lot more anger toward him.

All of the madness was created by one woman who chose to lie and then use the lie and the children as a means of manipulation fifteen years later. All of the heartbreak was shared by everyone involved except for the person who caused it. And all of the tears and pain I watched my husband go through, while I could do nothing to help him, ended in the Supreme Court. There was a child left with confusion and devastation to deal with over where he really came from or where he belonged. There was a man left childless after 15 years of being a father.

My husband won a lawsuit in Supreme Court with a verdict that the mother was to pay him back all of the money he had paid for medical bills and child support over the years based on her lie, which was labeled and proven as fraud. This was the first time in the United States that a verdict was issued to make a woman pay a man back child support that was court ordered to give her. But, even with the winning verdict, it was my husband and John who really lost. John lost the man he called daddy and my husband lost the boy he called son. We didn't continue on in court to make her pay back the money that the judges awarded my husband. We settled with the satisfaction of proving a point that if a woman can hide a secret and use it to destroy lives later on, then she should have consequences. But we did have wounds that we needed to work out with each other. The only good thing that came from those years was we gained out of the process a friendship with a lawyer who lost tons of money and time just for a cause that he believed in his heart was right. He was willing to help us because he believed we were good people. Things like that mean the most. I now joke with my husband that we are the only combined family that started out with three kids and are now down to one without anyone dying. Not a very nice joke, but true. And we were left with wounds that we once again had to find a way to heal.

Things were so bad at times that I longed to be back where I didn't belong, in Georgia. At least in Georgia I had roots and I could work without harassment and didn't have people lying about me or affecting my household with their manipulative ways. But the thought of moving back to everything I left behind and had wanted to run from in the first place always kept me in Tennessee. My husband and I went to marriage counseling, for the third time, to try to overcome the mistakes we had made toward one another once again. After many instances of wondering should I stay or should I go, I decided to stay to keep from moving my daughter and disrupting her life once again. We rebounded and started working on being a family again, made up of three people this time

instead of five.

WHEN THE HEART CAN'T FIND HOME

A few years after all the turmoil from the paternity issue had settled and we had pieced our family back together, I received a message from a guy who was my half- brother. He was now eighteen, but the last time I saw him was when he was six months old. He grew up where I was raised in Georgia and we shared the same father. He wanted to get to know me and he wanted to know why I didn't have anything to do with "our daddy" and "our family." As I sat and wrote a reply back to him stating that I had left home when I graduated high school and I didn't take the time to keep in touch with that side of the family as I probably should have, my husband looked at me confused. My husband asked me was I not going to share with my half-brother the real reason why. Was I not going to tell him what I had been told by the family over the years and exposed to during my years of childhood? Was I not going to tell him that when I did see 'our daddy' that he couldn't look at me, let alone have a conversation with me? I answered my husband with a no and explained that I was not going to share that

73

with him. He was raised very different than I was, so I thought why introduce him to the past now? As I waited for a reply back from my half -brother, I froze and my heart sank as I read the words, "I just don't understand how you can walk out on your family." There were so many different directions I could have gone with that one statement. There were so many different explanations and so many points I could have made and proven. But I didn't. I let it sink in and then I pushed it aside to the storage area in my mind of "reasons why I don't belong."

I wasn't a part of my family in Georgia and I didn't harbor the welcoming feeling in Tennessee, either. I started filtering thru a whirlwind of questions in my mind. How had I become in life to the point I am now? Why did I feel that my family in Georgia didn't want me? How did we get to this place in our life in Tennessee? I couldn't make my child suffer another move. I couldn't forgive my husband for the feelings of being put second and not standing up for me when his ex and his children were being rude to me. I was living in Tennessee and he had no desire to have a kid and refused to discuss it when I brought the subject up. At a time in my life when everything was supposed to be calm and peaceful, I still had sad emotions running in me that I could not resolve. Was this the life that God knew and intended for me to live when he created me? Was I the one always messing and scrambling everything up? Was there any place on this earth that I belonged. Is there someone who would respect me and be IN love with me, not just love me in a mediocre way or because they had an open spot to fill?

When you move around you get to experience the excitement that comes with new territory and meeting new people. But, thru the moving process you also tend to leave little pieces of yourself behind. I feel like I have lost parts of my identity because no one knows the whole me. I spent my childhood in a little community in Georgia, my early adulthood in North Carolina serving in the military, my days as a single parent in a different small community in Georgia, and now I have my life in Tennessee. I am thankful for all of my experiences and the people that I have met and shared my life with along the way. But, there is a bit of sadness from it that lingers in me and some days I continue asking the same question of myself: Will I ever find somewhere that I feel I truly belong or connect with someone that can combine each part of my life and process it enough to create an image of being able to see me whole?

Chapter Five

TRYING TO OUTDO MY PAST

The truth is, unless you let go, unless you forgive

yourself, unless you forgive the situation, unless you realize

that the situation is over, you cannot move forward.

-Steve Maraboli

I spend a lot of my vitality on my family and making sure

everything flows the way I feel it should. There have been times

that I spent the last ounce of energy and money I had to make sure

my daughter had the best birthday parties, Christmases' with

packages spread out under the tree and name-brand clothes. I paid

for private lessons to make her a better ball player, cheerleader,

and violin player. I stayed involved in her school activities and can

proudly say that she earned grades that put her in the top ten of her

graduating class. We did annual Easter-egg hunts and trick-or-

treating in town and celebrated everything we could celebrate. We still do. When she graduated high school she had a list of eight colleges to choose from that had accepted her, after I spent endless hours helping her fill out applications and forms so that she would have options and a choice.

She was raised in a nice home frequently full of friends laughing, eating, and hanging out just because they cherished being together. I had managed to shelter her from most of the arguments and the sadness that we went through and I put in extra efforts to make sure our problems did not affect her life or activities. I gave her the option of freedom of speech without consequences in our home and tried to make her realize that we can agree to disagree and I will love her no less. Our home was where her friends could gather to decorate homecoming floats, play flag football, lie on the trampoline and look up at the stars, or play in the creek on hot summer days. She had the experiences of lake trips, summertime at the river with boats and jet skis or fishing off the dock, vacations at the beach, weeklong cruises, and weekends camping and riding four-wheelers. I was referred to as mom by many of her friends. I was eagerly at her awards ceremonies, school functions, and events, usually embarrassing her by taking pictures and being teary-eyed or bragging about every little accomplishment she achieved. Her dad and I did not put her in the middle of our disagreements. We have proven many times that we can sit down and have a meal together and show her that we can be civil and she is our primary interest and greatest achievement. She has never had to pick sides or feel that she can't love both of us. Her stepdad would give her his last ounce of being to make sure she was happy. She has lost friends to death and endured heartbreaks over boys. I took her to counseling when devastation came about to make sure she had an outlet and someone to talk to. I have stayed up with her many nights trying to shoo away fears, pain, and tears. Has she faced hardships? Yes. Was I a perfect mother? Far from it. Did I give it everything I had to protect her and her well-being? Yes.

Though I have tried to shelter her and protect her, my heart sinks when I watch her sitting still and can see through her eyes that her mind is turning a hundred miles an hour. I cringe when I observe her walking with her shoulders slumped and her head down. I look at her and wonder if she is, also, cursed or damaged. Does she carry around inside of her the wheel that never stops turning? Does she have a regular feeling of being unsettled? She is beautiful inside and out and she carries inside her an old soul. She had a childhood and a high school résumé full of accomplishments that would make your head spin. But she leaves me wondering so often where her confidence was left and whether she is going to live a life based on uncontrolled emotions and overthinking. Will she be able to just let it all be? Will she deal on a daily basis with the feelings of the curse? Is it something that can be inherited and not just credited to misfortunes that happen in life?

When I refer to being damaged, I am referring to having feelings of condemnation, sorrow, guilt, pain, empathy, sympathy, betrayal, loss, not being accepted, or any particular emotion or combination of emotions. Things may cut you a little deeper than they do others. You may feel shackled by your sins and carry them embedded inside of you causing you insecurity. Or on a different

day you may feel so deep in thought and connected to yourself that

you feel overly excited and want to change the world in a day. You

can't find enough space to store half the energy you have bouncing

around in your mind and body. You want to create things and grow

and conquer. Every emotion is extreme, whether it is a good or a

bad emotion. You rarely ever get the pleasure of being able to

settle for mediocre.

THE CONVICTION OF THE CURSE

I shared all of my previous stories to lead up to the reason I felt compelled to sit and spill a few of my life's shortcomings out in a blubbering, jumbled mess on paper. I said all of that to say this: I am damaged. I am so damaged that some mornings I have to cover my head and lie in bed until I can talk myself in to getting up and brushing my teeth. I am damaged to the point that I can't deal with sitting still or excessive quietness for long periods of time. I need noise, music, and organized chaos stirring around me. My mind on a normal day has entertained more thoughts before nine o'clock in the morning than most people will process the entire day. I tell my husband that I want to quit work because I hate getting up in the morning and having to punch a time clock. My husband responds that his fear of my not working is that he would come home one day to the house torn apart and laid in piles of lumber in the yard because I got bored. I need interaction. I need a purpose. I need my time occupied. If I am not busy, then I leave the room for the curse to grow in my mind.

The curse is made up of different categories, and they do not have to take place in a certain order. One part of the curse is sleep, or the lack of. There are times when I unintentionally go days without sleeping. Several causes contribute to my occasional spells of insomnia, but I think the main one is that I love nighttime. Everything is more peaceful to me at night and I love to soak it in. I am a nocturnal creature and darkness makes me thrive on the inside. I can clean, paint, think, or consume my time with whatever I want and there is no other commotion about from anyone else to hinder me. I own all that is around me with no explanation to anyone. Night time is welcomed by me as the time that I can just be and there are no expectations to fill other than my own.

Another issue I face with sleep is that I often have recurring nightmares. When I awake from one then I usually do not go back to sleep for the rest of the night and I carry the troubled feelings it stirs with me for the rest of the day. I have the same feelings of being scared that I had as a child and the same sad emotions consume my thoughts until I can find something else to redirect or focus on. I feel the same dirtiness and unworthiness that I felt when I was younger and I was being touched inappropriately. I carry the same shame around until I can do or find something that makes me feel more positive or that I have a purpose.

Other times at nightfall my mind likes to wander and sometimes when everything is peaceful and quiet, it takes a stroll and often doesn't come back for hours. I get in my day dreaming mode and I can't remove myself from it enough for my thoughts to settle and fall asleep. This leads to another category of the curse: Fixation.

I get fixated on things and can waste an entire day pondering them. The situation doesn't have to be directly related to me. I take the phrase "Put yourself in someone else's shoes" to an entirely new level. My husband has made countless trips taking groceries to someone's home, dropping off bags of clothes, cutting firewood, or helping repair homes of people that we did not know personally. He does this so I can let the thoughts of their hardship go and not become fixated on it for days. When we see someone in need, a look comes across his face because he knows that we are about to get involved.

In one of my therapy sessions I was explaining that my brother had done something to upset my mother. I was in the process of buying him a bus ticket to come stay with me for a while to help get his issues resolved without my mother having to deal with it. The counselor looked at me and said, "Why?" I said, "because it will take the burden off of them." He said, "But why? You didn't create the problem. Why do you need to fix it?" That has stuck with me, and there are times that I have had to stop and say the very same thing to myself. Some things are not mine to fix. But it is hard to let stuff go when you also have what I like to call the sixth sense, which is also another category of the curse: Empathy.

Along with all of the other emotions I carry around, I also carry around feelings from others' misfortunes. If I see someone counting change or trying to figure out what they can afford in a store, I feel their worry. When someone is acting different and people cannot relate to them, I relate all too well. My thoughts go to my brother who has been diagnosed with schizophrenia over and over and I still to this day don't really know if I believe he is. I don't know if Cory is schizophrenic or if he is so full of the emotions that we were introduced to throughout life that his mind gets overtaken with thoughts that go so deep that he does not know how to process them. That leads me to wonder if am I schizophrenic and just never had the nerve to open up to someone enough to diagnose it.

Cory will make comments that can shoot straight to the core of my heart. "The pain of the Vietnam War didn't stop with the soldiers. We are a product of the suffering, too, Sis. We had to deal with a father who was a Vietnam Vet." When he makes those types of comments, he is not schizophrenic, he is wise. Actually, he is one of the smartest people I know. Others may see a drug addict or a person that has no control over his feelings and actions. I see a person who struggles emotionally and sits for hours at a time reading his Bible. My husband will ask me on occasion what is going on with my brother when Cory is in one of his overly talkative moods. My simplest reply is always, "He is just fighting demons." I know that he has sat and pondered a little too long and gone a little too deep and needs to talk his way back to calmness. Cory needs someone to say they understand the same way he understands so he isn't alone in his way of thinking. He needs to feel validated.

I have always understood that sympathy was when you feel bad for someone and empathy is when you have actually experienced the same pain. I listen to every word people say and sometimes I probably listen a little harder than I should. Not only do I listen and process what people say, I read their body language, face, and eyes. I know if they are uncomfortable, sad, annoyed, or happy. And if they appear to be anything but happy, then I feel we need to focus on what is making them unhappy and resolve it. Someone being uncomfortable makes me uncomfortable. Some people refer to this as having a sixth sense, a gut feeling, or being psychic. I think it is intuition that sharpens with each feeling you have to process through life.

The hardest phase to deal with in the curse process is the guilt stage. I am not referring to the guilt you feel because you did something wrong. I am talking about the guilt you carry because you let someone down or you question their actions. There is lingering guilt when I ask myself if my parents really loved me. I am asking because of some of their actions, but then I feel guilty because I would even think such a thing and devalue them in that way. I have guilt when I listen to my mother and wonder why she can't just be happy for one conversation or when I realize that I am barely listening to what she is saying. I stopped trying to have a relationship with my father years ago and that leaves guilt. I carry the guilt from feeling like they should have given me a little more to go on in life. There is even guilt for trying to live a fulfilling life with happiness. I feel like I don't deserve it at times or I am being selfish because there are so many others who have so much less than I.

There are many different phases and emotions of the curse. The only way I know to explain it is the feeling you have when you are standing on the beach in the sand and the waves are rolling over your feet. The sand is never still; it constantly shifts and moves under your feet. While the water is rushing in to shore and then scurrying back out to sea, you have a feeling of excitement stirring in you because you don't know if you are going to see something beautiful or if something not so welcoming is going to appear. You feel the motion of the sand washing away under your feet, you hear the sounds of the waves crashing, you feel the warmth of the water, and you are trying to see whatever Mother Ocean has brought into shore with her. All of your senses are in overdrive, and you don't know how to process it from one moment to the next. It is peaceful yet stirs excitement at the same time. That is how the curse leaves you. Not always bad, not always good, but your mind and senses are constantly in overdrive.

CAUSE AND EFFECT

People often refer to karma when they are trying to say that someone receives what they deserve as a result of their actions. I think we create our own karma. I believe in life coming "full circle," and I believe in "cause and effect." To me cause and effect is the simplest way to live in this world. But we have created a world where everyone makes excuses for the cause and intercepts and changes the effect. In my opinion, this makes the cycle warped. An example: A person acts as a bully. People shun the bully, advising the bully that this is not acceptable and will not be tolerated. This sends a message to the bully that what he was doing is wrong and the bully stops. The person they were bullying no longer has to deal with it and they realize there are people in the world that do care. The feeling of kindness from everyone helps to heal the wounds that the bully created for the victim. The bully becomes a better person because his actions were not tolerated. Everyone loves one another again and lives in harmony. A happy ending results due to cause and effect. In our current society it often plays out like this: A person is a bully. People either cower away because they do not want to get involved, or some start to join in. This brings the bully positive attention and reinforces the bully's actions. After all, the bully needs support and is justified in his actions because he is just acting out because he was fat as a child or still is, or one of a million other excuses. This sends a message to the person being bullied that it is acceptable and that others support the bully. This creates a sad, unhealthy social environment.

For most people it usually stops there, but not in my world. I see the bully, and it sends me over the edge and I sit and ponder the situation in my head and have to send it through my process. The end result usually plays out that when I get the first opportunity, I will tell the bully he or she is a bully and all the people that condoned it are not worth very much, either. Then I am labeled as a person who has an attitude. And after I feel relieved because I got to have my say comes the same comment from my husband, "Why did that matter so much to you? Why couldn't you just know that they were a bully and leave it alone?" Then there I go back to the process of the curse. Why did that matter to me? It mattered to me because I cared about someone's well-being, which leads me to wonder why others didn't care about the person's well-being. And then the process starts over again. One of my friends explains me by saying I am just "passionate." I know she is being way too kind with that description, but I will take it. It is way nicer than some of the words that others have used to describe me.

This is the process that I live with every day. When I watch the news, when I watch TV, when I watch a movie, when I see someone hurting, this is the process of my mind. When I hear someone speak badly of someone and then turn around and cover them with kindness, I have to go through the process. Others just say, "Oh, they are two-faced" and move on. Not me. I need to know why they are two-faced. Why didn't they just tell the other person how they really felt and deal with it? Does this person do the same to me? Well, let me ask them. And then here we go again.

By now, I am sure it seems to you that I love conflict. It is actually the opposite. I don't do well with negative, drama-filled situations. When I have to deal with those situations I usually add to the drama because of my "passionate" personality. I don't let things go until I feel that they are resolved. I love to laugh and create a bond with my friends. I get a euphoric effect for days after I share a bout of laughter or a good time with someone. I don't forget it. I cling to it and I appreciate it. It changes me on the inside. But when I see someone being mistreated, I tend to be passionate in my choice to defend them, also. I run on emotions and need justification or answers. I have to rationalize myself and the world around me.

I worked in a neurology office at one of the top teaching universities in the US, and the staff became like family. We made the best out of our workdays and shared pretty much everything and accepted each other with no restrictions. We always tried to outdo one another no matter whether it was eating, telling a joke, doing a better job, or pulling the best prank. And when someone told a story, someone else would tell a story to outdo it. After working beside these people for a year, I started opening up about a few of my past situations, and on occasion I would tell a childhood story to try to outdo one of my coworkers' stories. One day I was in a story match with one of the doctors. After he shared a situation he survived that he thought was rather sad, I shared a situation I survived that I felt had more sadness than his. After I was finished telling my story, he was looking at me and offered no words. I said, "Crazy, huh?" He replied, "Not just that, I am just sitting here wondering how you are walking around and functioning normally in society." We both started laughing, and went on about our day. I stored that in my "I am worthy" file.

When abusive things happen to you, it sets you apart from others in your mind. You develop a sense of being less valuable than those who may not have been exposed to such things. You feel tarnished, for a lack of a better word. After the situations pass, you are left alive with an emotional aftermath that could never be explained on paper. Then you feel like you are even more abnormal for having these deep emotions. When I refer to my "I am worthy file," I mean that I am justified in having these different emotions and it doesn't mean that something is wrong with me. It is normal to feel the way I do at that time due to what I have faced in the past. I could be totally off on that logic, but it works for me. On days I can't seem to calm my mind and I start feeling like a roller coaster is going nonstop in my head, I pull that file out and I can laugh and feel a little justification for my madness and move on. I am cursed with the need to rationalize the simplest things, and I have to make sure I deserve goodness or I come to a point where I conclude that I deserve sorrow for something. You often hear people say everything happens for a reason. I need to know the reason. I also have to talk myself into letting things go. To some people that is an easy thing to do, but I have to really work on it. I live with conviction every day, whether it be my own or someone else's.

Chapter SIX

USING MY CONTROL TO OVERRIDE

YOURS

There are wounds that never show on the body that
are deeper and more hurtful than anything that bleeds.
-Laurell K. Hamilton

I have always been convinced that people control us more than we
know. Being a pleaser leaves you spending a lot of your time
prioritizing others' emotions over your own. Growing up with
abusive or narcissistic parents teaches you all too well how to
become compliant. I have spent most of my life with my mother
controlling my actions by her reactions. I watched every word I
said to her because I felt I should say what she wanted me to and
not what I was thinking or really felt. If I do or say something she
doesn't like or I don't respond the way she wants, then she

punishes me by shutting me out or acting like I don't care about her. If I don't call her as quickly or as often as she thinks I should, then she will not answer when I do call. When she decides to answer, she will be short with her responses or let me know how rough her life is and that I am not there for her.

Our conversations usually start out the same each time. "Hey Mama, how are you?" She responds, "Not good. I am hurting." I then say, "I wish there was something that could help you." Then comes her most common reply," I am just living in hell." The conversation then turns to my listening to her talk for a while about how everyone uses her, how there is no one to help her or be there for her, she is all alone, or she just can't take it anymore. If she doesn't get an acceptable reaction from me with those comments then she will move on to they may lose their home or they don't have any food to eat in the house. I know their home is paid for and they keep groceries well stocked. If I say my head has been hurting then she will inform me that her head has hurt for years. If I say I am tired, then she replies that she hasn't been able to get out of bed for months. Everything is tragic in her world and she wants my responses to be filled with sadness for her. And for a long time she has had me trained well.

A few years ago my husband told me that he can tell when I have talked to my mother because of the way I act with sadness or angry emotions after she and I have a conversation. I pondered what he said and questioned why I let my mother control my emotions. I don't live in the same state as her and she still leaves me feeling like a three-year-old who needs to please her or have her approval. So after a while of pondering, I decided to start talking to her like I would talk to anyone else: normally. If she called and I was busy then I would not answer the phone. If our conversations started turning to negative things I would dismiss it and try to direct it to something more pleasant. She always found a way to bring the conversation back to the negative. I tried to have a solution for every negative thing she brought up. If she was hurting, I encouraged her to get out of the bed every so often and walk a short distance to build her muscles up. I explained to her that lying in bed would make anyone hurt. She would then respond that she couldn't and I didn't understand how bad it hurt her to walk. I told her to try physical therapy. She stated that made her pain worse than it already was. If she complained of feeling lonely or depressed, I would suggest she take short drives with Papa to get out of the house. Her rebuttal was they couldn't because he drove like a bat out of hell and scared her. Finally, after many conversations in which all my suggestions were met with negative excuses, I suggested to her that maybe she needed to start smoking pot. That would increase her appetite, she wouldn't feel as much pain, she would be more relaxed emotionally, and she wouldn't care how bad Papa drove when they went somewhere. I explained that it would really be a win-win situation if she woke up and took a hit of a joint before she started her day. Of course that led to her not talking to me for a while, but when I hung up the phone, I didn't have the urge to slam my head against the wall. I was actually smiling.

I had to learn that I did not have to feed into the fact that she felt her life was miserable. I had to reprogram myself to accept that when she was down and low, it was okay that I wasn't. I had to accept that she is making a choice to live that way, but I do not have to. I am allowed to be happy, even if she is not.

It is not an easy process to overcome. It means that I will have to deal with a lot of mixed emotions and the aftermath of guilt when I know that I have upset her. But it was a decision I had to make for my own sanity. There are occasions now when she states she is living in hell and I reply that it seems she always has. When she tries to bring up the past, I tell her that I don't want to talk about it. And when she is complaining of her pains, I cut the conversation short and tell her to call me when she feels better. I had to grasp that I am an adult now, just as she is, and I am not responsible for the misery that she feels. But the hardest thing that I had to comprehend and accept was the fact that things will never get any better. I will never have carefree conversations with my mother and she will probably never be happy. After I accepted that fact, I gave her ownership of her emotions and I took back ownership of mine. The saying "It is what it is" really does have value and brings with it some relief when you accept it as the truth when dealing with situations that you cannot control.

SCARS THAT DON'T HEAL

Scars are a unique thing. You have skin to protect your body. After you damage your skin and it heals, there is often a scar left. The scar is visible so people can see that at one time there was a wound there, but your body is healed and you are no longer at risk for infection. Your skin is in a sense whole again. Scars that go deeper and are formed on your heart don't heal so easily.

I don't know if it is scars I carry on my heart, or just deep-rooted grudges. I still have issues with my mother. The older my daughter gets, it seems the deeper the issues go and the more I question my upbringing. My mother has told me time after time that she did the best she could or knew how to do when she was raising us. She could always rationalization why my pain was due to someone else and how she suffered more than I. There are times when I am talking about my love for my daughter and mama will respond with that is how she feels about me. This should be something that I love to hear and makes my day brighter, but instead I cringe and it makes me feel a little madness stirring inside. I have lived my adult life trying to raise my daughter differently than I was raised and protecting her from the hurt that was in my control. At nine years old I was burdened with cleaning house, washing clothes, making supper for Cory and I, and making sure everything was in order when Mama came home from work at midnight. Cory and I got ourselves up and dressed and left for school on our own. So, when my mother compares her love for me to the love I feel for my child, I start thinking of all the circumstances I was exposed to and all of the things that went awry. I start questioning how she could have let those situations happen. I compare what I faced in my childhood to the way I raised my daughter. I have to process all of that and usually conclude that there is no way my mother could even love me, much less adore me the way I do my child. After I come to my conclusion, I then move on to the next stage: Guilt.

I feel guilty for thinking of my mother in such a way. She provided us with a home. She would come have lunch with me at school occasionally because she couldn't be at home at night because she was working. I have observed her more than once battered and crying after being beaten. I have spent nights in bed in the darkness listening to her scream and cry while she was trying to protect herself. I have watched her as she walked in to the local store and asked to borrow money so that we could purchase food for that week. Then my mind will wander off to the years of her staying up late at night and welcoming my teenage friends into our house and sitting and laughing with us. I think of the days we went to the lake and sat and talked for hours. I look back to the weekends of us landscaping the yard or picking strawberries out of the strawberry patch. I call to mind her working overtime to buy me my first horse and a moped when she was nowhere near able to afford it. I do have some very fond memories of my mother, but all of those disappear when I hear her say that one sentence. I don't know if it is because I think she is dismissing the way I was brought up. That would be an odd reason to me, because I loathe thinking about those days. I don't know if I get so exasperated because I tried to raise my child totally different. I don't know why

I get so irritated when she declares she loves me the way I love my child. But I do know why I feel so guilty. I feel guilty because in the very core of my being, I know that she thinks she did the best she could, but I feel that it wasn't satisfactory enough.

I get the same feeling when my mother states that she doesn't want to do to me what her mother did to her. My granny was a pessimist as well. I have lived in a different state for eleven years and Mama and Papa have come to visit me twice. It is not because we don't keep in touch. We talk several times a week. It is because my mother has been disabled since I was fifteen and I can't remember one day in my later years that my mother didn't have pain. When events take place, not only do I know that she will not be present, I also know that she will call crying and upset on the day of the event to tell me how she has to suffer and what she misses out on in life because of her disability. When she starts crying and asking me for confirmation that she was a good mother, it starts a fire in me. When my parents call and say they miss me it makes my heart ache because I miss them. And then I feel angry because I don't understand why they can't come see my world. I feel guilty because I don't go home like I used to and like I should. I feel guilty because my parents are getting old and I am not there to help them. I feel guilty for wondering why I should. Then I see her hurting. She is always so fragile and always in pain whether it is emotionally or physically. The smallest things are upsetting to her. I still don't have answers to questions regarding Mama, and I am not sure that I ever will. I try to believe that she loves me the best way she knows how. But, I also know how much I love my child and am left to wonder about a lot of things.

My father apparently changed when he started his new family. He raised his youngest sons a bit different than Cory and I. I stopped trying to talk to him for many years because he never seemed to know what to say. Now he is older and has health issues and when I get phone calls informing me that he is very sick, I have no idea where to go with it. My mind is filled with questions such as: Do I have a right to care? Do I try to talk to him now? If he dies, will I be asked to leave the funeral home? Will I even go to the funeral home? I believe he loves me, and I feel that he doesn't say much to me because he probably has no idea what to say. I know he was a freshly returned Vietnam Veteran when we were together as a family. I know he carries guilt. But then I think of the new family he created and the two boys he raised totally differently than we were and without all of the dysfunction. I feel hurt and I don't understand why they deserved better than Cory and I did. Daddy can have a conversation with Cory and they keep in touch. But, I still don't know why he can't even say he loves me before we hang up the phone the one time a year we may talk.

All of the things regarding my parents leave me with so many questions. How did I become an adult and neither of my parents have a clue about my current life? Why can't I call just one of my parents and have a normal conversation? Why does my mother always want me to feel sorry for her? Why am I expected to comfort them when I didn't feel comforted during my worst moments?

One definite truth is there are some scars we don't outgrow and sometimes wounds come back as fresh and painful as the day they were created. I also know how hard it is to process guilt that you feel is really due to others' adversity. And feeling that your guilt is due to someone else's actions causes even more guilt when it is someone that you love. Granny always said to me when I acted sassy, "Baby girl, do not get above your raising." If Granny only knew that as hard as I try to get above it, I never foresee a day that it will ever happen.

Chapter Seven

MANAGING THE MADNESS

I may fall apart but I will never lose the pieces. I will

always see the picture that they create, and my hands

bloody, cracked, trembling, and tired, will never stop

fumbling to put them back together.

-Tyler Knott Gregson

THE PAST

I am going to share with you a secret that took me a long time to

realize, accept, and believe. There are still days that I have to

advise myself this over and over. It is something that resolves so

many issues and makes the largest impact on one's life, but yet is

the hardest thing for a person to come to grips with. It takes

practice, but it really requires no effort except to say it and believe

it. "THE PAST IS THE PAST." Five words that can change you

and your future in more ways than anything else you can do in your life. But you have to cover yourself with it and own it for it to be effective. A person can have a habit for twenty years, decide on one night that they do not want to partake in the habit any longer, and that is it. It is now a part of the past. It is done, resolved, and no longer having any control over that person. What I have done, what I have been through, what I used to be means nothing now when I simply say that it is in the past. So first and above all else, take the hurt and the sadness and the things that hold you back or give you an ounce of insecurity and declare them no more because that is a closed chapter in your life and it is now a part of your past. I have learned over time that when I have moments of questioning and searching for answers that don't exist, sometimes I have to just rationalize it all with "The past is the past."

WE ARE ALL IMPERFECT

The next secret that I am going to share is this: NO ONE IS PERFECT. Not one single soul walking on this earth is without a mistake. You are not going to think or do one thing that has not been explored before by another human being. The only difference is that some people are secure enough to admit it.

I was talking with a friend whom I have only known in our adult life, and the entire time I have known her she has been pretty much perfect. This lady is active in the church, constantly devotes her time to others and charities, volunteers at the family center, married only once and is still married after twenty-three years. This is a woman I call when I am in an evil mood because I know she will see the good side of something and help me make better decisions. This woman, who is very much respected and well known in the community, was telling me of her younger days that involved getting high and dating a drug dealer. I developed new admiration for her because she was secure enough to share something with me that I would have never known or guessed. She made an impact on me not by being perfect, but by being real.

This belief has also been confirmed for me many times by my neighbors. We like to have gatherings at our house, and most of the time they are loud. At any given time there could be five or six cars in our yard, and people come and go frequently. My neighbor is a preacher. While we are watching a football game in the garage with our loud friends, they may be at the neighborhood creek baptizing someone. I can honestly say that through the years of being blessed with them living beside us and our kids being best friends and going through school together, I have never felt one ounce of judgment from them. They make me want to do better and be a better person not because they lecture or correct me, but because they accept me for being me. They don't expect me to be perfect or live the same as they do, but yet they treat me and my family as if we are perfect and we are all the same. I see God in their daily lives more than I have ever felt at a sermon in church. I can call them with any need or any question, and they do the same in return. They are real and they don't pretend not to be.

I lived a long time comparing myself to others and feeling that I came up a little less worthy. It took me a while to realize that admitting your mistakes and knowing they do not define you in the present is one of the best things you can do for yourself. It gives you freedom. We are all the same, and sometimes when you admit you have made mistakes and are not perfect, it makes the load you carry a little bit lighter. If someone acts like they don't have skeletons in their closet, they are carrying a heavier load than you and I. Love yourself and try to laugh at your shortcomings if they don't hurt others. I have learned to laugh at myself frequently and admit that I am not perfect, nor will I waste my time trying to be.

I work with a nurse who is the total opposite of me. She is quiet, tolerant of others, and very reserved in her opinions. A few years ago she would have intimidated me. Now I stick to being myself and I tell her that God brought her to me to keep me in line. We spend our days in the same office laughing and with my spouting off what are usually inappropriate comments and her smiling because inside I know she agrees or was thinking it herself and is too well mannered to voice such things. I will say or do something absurd and then look at her and tell her she is failing at her job of helping me be a better person. Her response is usually, "You really don't give yourself enough credit." You don't make people happier by putting them down or being above them. You bring people peace by being real and sometimes a little imperfect. We all fall short in the eyes of God. Believe it.

THERAPY

One of the most underused resources in dealing with life is
therapy. People will comment that they need therapy, but rarely
does one seek therapy to help resolve issues they are facing. I was
explaining to someone who was experiencing a hard time in her
marriage that therapy really helped me and my husband. She
looked at me shocked and said that she would have never thought
we went to therapy because we seem so happy. I told her we are
happy, but at a couple of different points in our relationship we
didn't like each other very much. In the past I had my hesitations
with therapy and did not want to carry the label or be judged by
others for needing assistance. I actually told my husband the first
time we went together that if the therapist told me that I was the
one to blame or that I needed to change something, I would
probably punch both of them in the face. I didn't need one more
person telling me I was wrong about something. At the end of the
therapy session the counselor looked at my husband and said that
he had a lot of work to do and gave him three things he needed to

work on before our next meeting. Then she advised me that I was not at a point that she could give me an assignment; she just hoped that I would return for the next session. Having a person who was neutral and wanted the best for both of us changed our marriage and our actions. The therapist was able to point out in a civilized, unaccusing manner what our issues were and make suggestions on how to go about trying to understand and respect one another so we could work on our differences.

I have used therapy at different points in my life. Sometimes I didn't feel it helped and thought maybe I knew more than the therapist did. Other times I have felt it changed my entire situation. I have used therapy for my daughter to have an outlet. When she came home after a couple of sessions and I saw no improvement, instead of giving up, I switched her to a different therapist. Not only is it important to go to therapy, it is also important to find the correct therapist. It costs good money to see a therapist, so find one that you feel is really helping you, not just asking questions that make you feel cloudier inside. A good sign that you have found the right person is that when you leave, you are already looking forward to your next session. Trust me on that—I know therapy well.

MEDICATION

My next suggestion for dealing with raging emotions is a controversial one, but I have to put it out there. Medicate. I am not talking about illegal drugs or alcohol (though there have been occasions when a good cold beer has really helped me put things in perspective). I am talking about prescription medications that were invented with the intention of serving as antidepressants. Medication is at the top of the list with the therapy sessions for making people feel labeled or abnormal for needing to use them. I myself have fought that battle. When I was in nursing school and going through my divorce, I worked with a physician who offered me medication. I took him up on his suggestion, and after trying different types, I found one that worked for me. I took it for a while and then decided that I didn't need it. I didn't want to be on a prescription drug for the rest of my life. When my husband I went through our hard times and the child paternity issue, I took it again. My "OCD issues" then turned into "whatever, I don't really care issues" and my family had a hard time accepting my new attitude. So, I again stopped taking it.

We spent a lot of time during my daughter's senior year visiting colleges and attending their football games or events. It was my goal for my daughter to find the place she wanted to be and move there and thrive. She picked the university that she liked, and we started preparing. I was so proud of her and wanted her to have the full college experience. It was also during this time that I diagnosed myself with having a mental breakdown. I couldn't look at her without crying and thinking I was losing my identity. I had no idea what I was going to do with my time now that we didn't have football games, softball games, basketball games, and all of her functions to base our life around. I couldn't get past the worries that someone might try to hurt her, and I could not accept her being in the world without me near her. This was the moment in her life that I had raised and prepared her for. I wanted her to have the opportunities and knew without a doubt that she needed to grow into her own being, but I was stuck in my selfishness and how it was going to change my world. Her friends spent a great deal of the summer before she left at our house, and I couldn't talk to them without crying, because all I could focus on was that my house was going to be quiet without them running in and out all of the time. As the time for her to leave got closer, I took heed of some of my friends' suggestion that I might need to get some help. I did, and I went back to taking my medication.

A few months later my daughter hated being away from home, moved back and picked a closer college. The doctor asked me at my checkup if I wanted to stop taking the medication since she was coming back home. I said, "Nah, I am good." I had reached a point in my life where I was able to accept that I felt better taking a pill every day than trying to control my emotions without it. Now, I ask myself why I did not stick with it sooner.

After I went back to taking my medication, I was working with a physician who was one of the nicest people I had ever met. He had a great work ethic and was very humorous most of the time. But, there were times when things would happen and he would get what I considered overly upset. He was always worried about upsetting someone or something not being right and he questioned himself a lot. So I started telling him often that antidepressants were really a good thing. A few months later I noticed he was calmer about things and did not get upset nearly as much. One day I told him that antidepressants really looked good on him. He started laughing and said that he had indeed started taking it and he felt better. I also noticed more of his patients were calling in asking for their antidepressant refills.

I am not trying to advertise for drug companies. I am trying to make a point that sometimes we need a little help. I am trying to convey that it doesn't mean you are weak or abnormal. I don't like depending on drugs, and I sure don't support narcotics or street drugs for a high (except for my mother—I still swear that marijuana would work wonders for her emotionally). But, I do think that if you are an emotional wreck on a constant basis, then maybe antidepressants are an option for you to explore.

MUSIC

I have an obsessive need for music. I remember events in my life, feelings, and people through music. I can tell you what song was playing the first time I kissed a boy, the first time I danced at a school function, or at about any phase of my life. I am the person pulling in the parking lot at work in the morning with the radio blasting like a sixteen-year-old riding around on a Friday night. If I hear a song and I feel a connection to it, I can play it over and over all day long. I listen to the words and dissect the song into a million different pieces. Music is appropriate for any occasion. It is like reading a book; it can entertain your mind and take you to a different place for a little while. Music can be great therapy.

FRIENDS

One of the best rewards you can give yourself is finding a true friend. I am not referring to the people you come in contact with every day and smile and say hi or have conversations because you are sitting at the same ball field or work at the same job. I am talking about the one person who would be happy for you if you won a million bucks or sad for you if you gained three pounds before a big event. I am talking about a person who doesn't feel the need to compete with you, doesn't call just when they want something, knows when you need space or when you don't. I know that it seems impossible to find someone with those qualities, but it is possible. I have made my share of enemies with my passionate personality, but I have to say that I am beyond blessed with friends. There have been days that I felt like I could tear the world in half in a matter of minutes, and I call a friend to have dinner and it changed my entire spirit. My friends possess their own uniqueness and I feel that keeps me well rounded.

There are so many friends that play a different role in my life and each one of them is special to me for that role. Every one of my closest friends gives me something that no one else can. I also know that I put a lot of responsibility on my friends because of what my definition of friendship is. But, I also want to be to them what they are to me. I pride myself in my friends because when I look at them, I know that I have the best of the best. I know that we all want to surround each other and lift each other up, no matter how different our personalities are. I am more than blessed to have the people that I share my life with surrounding me.

CREATE YOUR SUPERPOWER

I was born with absolutely no talent whatsoever. I have nothing about me that stands out or that I can do better than anyone else. I am not graced with good looks, I can't sing, I can't dance, I don't play an instrument that amounts to anything that could be classified as music. I am not overly intelligent and I excel at no sport. I am not artistic because my OCD will not let me be creative because I need things to be simple and organized. I spent most of my life on the sidelines because I was not confident or graceful enough to be in the game. I am the definition of average. The two best qualities that I possess are my imagination and my gift of daydreaming. I probably excel at those two things enough to rank me as exceptional.

When we moved to Tennessee, I was one of the loneliest people on the planet. I had no hobbies and no friends to talk to. To say the least, the women in the town we moved to were not welcoming. After being here a while I did make a couple of friends through our children and their activities and a few of our neighbors who were our age. So, I started having gatherings and using my imaginative superpower to plan events. I love to give a theme to everything. To attend one of my events you might be asked to wear a wig, dress like a rock star, or whatever I have going through my head at the time. I always plan games to play at our gatherings, whether it is trying to pop a balloon tied to someone's back or leg, playing Family Feud or spoons or trying to get the most toilet paper rolls on a plunger between your legs. Our gatherings turned into annual events and grew from six or eight people to anywhere from fifteen to thirty. Flag football games turned into the Turkey Bowl every Saturday after Thanksgiving. They come complete with banners to run through and trophies given to the captain of the winning team and the MVPs. We now have the annual Christmas party, New Year's Eve party, and Fourth of July party. I have even hosted a couple of adult proms at my house. Planning events is my superpower. I love it because it gives me something to do with my mind. While all my other friends may have been born with a gift or a natural superpower, I had to create mine, and I must say I am one

pretty dang good party planner.

FIND YOUR PERSON

I joke about a lot of things, and I find it easier to be aggravating than serious most of the time. But this is one thing that I am totally serious about and there is no joke. Other than religious choices, choosing who you will spend the rest of your life with is the biggest decision that you will ever make. Be very cautious when choosing your person. You are investing everything that you have in another human being. You are sharing your body, heart, soul, home, money, and one day possibly children with a person who is supposed to stand by you for the rest of your life. This is the person you have to look at on a daily basis, wash their nasty clothes, smell their foul odors when you walk in the bathroom as they are sitting on the toilet, listen to them blow their nose and watch snot drip from it when they are sick. Your person will also have to deal with you in the same instances in return. Your person should not have any desire to break you down, make you feel insecure or unworthy, harm you physically or mentally. Your person is the one that will be raising your children, so pick them with your future or maybe current children in mind.

Will they make a good mother or daddy? Will they support your family and be the backbone of your safe haven? Will they protect and give you courage, or will they tear you down and threaten you? Will they trust you enough to let you make your own decisions and have your own space, or will they control you and every aspect of your life? Do they already have issues that you have to deal with that effect you personally? Have they already disrespected you at some point and made you lose trust? When other people admire you or show you attention, does your person get jealous, or do they smile knowing that you are beautiful and you belong to them? When you can't make a monthly bill or have financial trouble, will they bail or will they stick by you and try to lessen the burden? If you lose everything you own, will they help you start over? Is this the man that you want to mold your son after? Is this the woman virtuous enough to raise you daughter? Does your person use your shortcomings against you, or do they help you find ways to conquer them and move forward? If your person has to spend time away from you, can they be trusted? Will they trust you? Are you going to spend your evenings laughing and talking about your days in full detail without having to sugar-coat or hide anything, or will you spend them explaining and making excuses to calm their insecurities? Do you feel blessed to have this person, and does this person feel blessed to have you? When the world attacks you, is this person going to defend you? When you are at your worst, is this person going to hold it against you?

If you can answer most of these questions, not just one or two or some, on a positive note, then you have found your person. Life is hard enough without it also being hard in your safe haven, your home. I am not implying that there will not be hard times. I am saying there is someone out there who will help you grow, love you to the moon, and make the fights worth it. Do not sell yourself short when you are deciding who will be your person, and pick a person who doesn't feel that they have settled for less either.

EXPLORE AND DARE TO LIVE

I realize that I fall short in many qualities. I have always fought with confidence or the lack of it. I need security, and I usually thrive only when I am in my comfort zone. But the one quality I do possess that arouses without needing persuasion is my need to explore. I can easily put off going to the grocery store in the town that I live in because I don't want to deal with other people, but put me in new surroundings, and I will soar. I love going to festivals and quaint little towns or being somewhere new and wandering around with no agenda. I love to walk the creeks and streams or lie on the ground in an open field. I love learning about different cultures and people's history. I watch a parade, and I am sure to cry because the universal happiness overwhelms me. This gets my husband every time. I can't help it. I soak it all in. I don't know if it is all connected to my big imagination or if I really contain a gypsy soul, but I love knowing that there is a large world out there and I will never be able to conquer all of it. There is always more waiting.

One time Sandy and I were on a road trip to New York. We didn't arrive at our destination on time, so my mother decided to report us missing. While Mama was contacting everyone and telling them we were probably kidnapped or dead, we were on the sidewalk in Gettysburg, Pennsylvania, watching the Fourth of July parade. Sandy and I got into an argument when we passed Washington, DC, over whether it was really the White House we just saw or was it located in Washington State. This led us to do a short tour to try figure out which one of us was right. The tour ended with us figuring out we were a little off track when we reached Baltimore, Maryland. While finding our way back to where we were supposed to be, we went through a town where everyone was lining up on the streets dressed in long flowing dresses and bonnets and Confederate uniforms. We had to stop because I absolutely love parades, and I am sure one of my ancestors was a Confederate soldier. This made us six hours late arriving in New York and presumed dead by my mother. But to this day, that was still the best parade I have ever witnessed.

Whatever location I am in, I become a local. I go to Key West, and I swear I am an islander. I go to the Cherokee reservation, and I swear I am Indian. Wherever I go, I usually leave thinking, "Yeap, that had to be where my ancestors came from." I spent one evening on Bourbon Street in New Orleans dancing in a conga line running a metal spoon up and down a washboard hanging on my chest thinking, "Yep, I must be Cajun." I often try to speak in accents trying to be funny. The physicians I worked with told me one day that it was the worst accent they had ever heard. They described it as a mixture of southern redneck, British, Jamaican, and Australian. I have no idea of my ancestry. Other than my parents, the only other forebearer of mine that I met was my maternal grandmother, who had wiry, unmanageable orange hair. I am pretty confident that she didn't come from an island or an Indian Village. And, the only thing I know that I inherited from my ancestors is my wiry, uncontrollable hair; a trait that I passed on to my daughter. I am sure it is because we are part Jamaican.

One thing you have to learn when you explore new territory is to act like you are amazed and a little ignorant. That usually intrigues whoever is from the area and makes them want to show or tell you more. That is how I hooked up with a nice accommodating Cajun lady who took me under her wing on Bourbon Street and showed me all the happening spots and things you have to try to connect to your real Cajun inner being. But, you cannot be shy when you are exploring. You have to be willing to try almost anything. This willingness is what led to the hurricane I drank that led to the dancing and playing spoons on a washboard.

My husband swears that I lose all my common sense of reality when I explore. We can be somewhere unfamiliar, and while he is scoping out the scenery and making sure we are safe, I am sightseeing, asking strangers questions, and trying to interact with the locals. This may have caused some tension between us when we were in the Bahamas. I love new territory. It doesn't even have to be somewhere far away. I was introduced to a small winery a few miles from where we live. Later, I found out that they have a band on Friday nights, and you can sit outside in the open air and listen to the music. What better way to explore my Italian side? Some girls and I packed up a tote with napkins, tablecloths, sliced up some cheddar cheese, grabbed some crackers, chocolate candy bars, wine glasses, and off we went in our highly fashionable tunics and boots. I am not sure that we qualified as cultured Italians after some of our group kept going on stage and singing with the band as the rest of us cheered them on while we danced from one end of the platform to the other. But, I can say that I had a great night doing something that was a little out of my element. It didn't make my husband very proud when he came to pick us all up at the owner's request and he could hear us screaming and singing as he pulled in the vineyard. But I told him not to worry: there was another vineyard down the road that we had not been to yet.

There is something about being in new territory that refreshes my soul and brings me contentment and peace. Learn to explore and open your mind up to new things. And do it with the utmost confidence and the mind-set of a child who soaks it all in and plays along. I tell my daughter constantly that there is a big world out there that stretches far from where we live our everyday lives, and with it comes new things and new people. When my daughter tells me that she is going to the Hippie Farm or take a hike up to Rattlesnake Falls, I smile because it tells me that she also has that gypsy spirit needing to be fulfilled.

FIND CLOSURE

This is a tricky part of moving on with your life. I always believed that you could only forgive people when they apologized and everyone hugged and made up and all was happy again. That belief left me carrying around a lot of open wounds and hurt. I am still working on how to have graceful closure of upsets in my life, but I am better at it than I used to be. People will not always apologize, nor will they always give you the ending that you want. But that doesn't mean that you can't find a way to find peace and move on. Sometimes there is closure in just deciding that for you, it is over.

I will probably never see the day that my father and I sit down and discuss why we have been strangers for so many years. But I did go and see him recently, and I left knowing that no matter what happens, I am at peace. He didn't kiss me or tell me that he loved me, but what could possibly be our last conversation and face to face meeting was enough for me to accept that it is what it is and I did what I needed to do to feel settled inside. We have had recent contact with the son my husband lost because of paternity issues and we have sat down and talked. We mourned thru the loss of a grandparent together. We may never have the same relationships that were lost, but we did find closure and all of us are learning how to communicate with our new selves. You cannot control others' actions, nor should you waste any of your time trying. You can control your actions, and that should be your focus. I have lost friends who talked about me or tried to hurt me later. In the past I would try to argue or defend myself. Now, more often than not, I let it go. I have got to a point in my life where I am happy. I don't care what others think, nor do I feel the need to explain myself. If you truly know me, then you know that I would never intentionally hurt someone. If you don't know that about me, then you don't know me well enough for me to be concerned with your opinion of me.

Time has a way of working things out and showing people's true colors. Let time do her thing. If you wrong someone, admit it and apologize and don't be the bitter soul. If someone wrongs you, let them be, and it will all work out in the end. I used to think that losing someone I considered a friend was a mark against me. I realize now that it is sometimes a blessing. You don't need relationships with the wrong people. The people who truly love you will find their way back.

SEARCH FOR THE CALM IN THE STORM

Everything will pass. I know this is easier to say than to believe. But it is the truth. Find your peace. I used to associate being by myself with loneliness. Now, I embrace the time I have by myself and welcome it. I always have projects going on and time alone is when I focus my attention on those. I am notorious for painting rooms in my home. My husband can go out of town on a business trip for a few days and return to several redecorated or repainted rooms. If I don't feel like doing something that requires manual labor, I read. When I am about two chapters into a good book, I could care less what is going on in the world around me. When something is going on that creates stress in your life, readjust your focus. Focus on something else that brings you peace. If someone is pressuring you into something you are unsure of, be bold enough to say that you need more time. If you have unsettled emotions, turn up the music and busy yourself with something that you feel is productive. Rearranging a closet or reorganizing cabinets can cure a bad set of nerves almost instantly. Do something nice for someone else. Make yourself available to help others. Only the things that you allow can entertain your thoughts. No matter what is going on in your life, always find something good to focus your attention on.

Chapter Eight

REBUILDING YOUR WORLD

"Never be afraid to fall apart because it is an

opportunity to rebuild yourself the

way you wish you had been all along."

-Rae Smith

I am no therapist, nor hold any licenses that certify me as capable of giving advice to anyone. I have nothing to prove my theories except my own perceptions and experiences. I have probably left more people confused than I have helped, and I stay in a state of confusion myself sometimes. But I tell you this and hope that you find enough trust in yourself to believe it: you are responsible for your world. Tear down every wall and remove every stepping-stone and start over if need be. If that doesn't work, do it again. Keep doing it until you can wake up one day and know that no matter what happens, you are going to be okay.

First, be honest with yourself. What feeds your insecurities? What harms you? What do you need to change that you can control? Change it. What do you need to change that you can't control? Get away from it. What do you need to do to resolve haunting issues from your past? Resolve it. Then, move forward. I used to be quick to spout off if someone was doing something to agitate me or that I disagreed with. I knew that I needed to calm myself in these instances and find different ways to react. I realized that my anger is just that, MINE. If I didn't want to feel anger, I needed to stop being angry.

I worked with a woman who was always smart and matter-of-fact with her words. I overlooked it at first, and then I tried to be kinder to her. It finally got to a point that when she started being dramatic, I wouldn't respond at all. I would look at her with no expression whatsoever, and after she rambled on for a bit and I didn't respond, she would finally stop and get back to the issue at hand. Let people know that you will not participate in drama. Let people know that you are happy and that you want happy vibes.

Sometimes even asking someone if there is something you can do to help them calm down and feel better will change the situation.

Search for what makes you happy, not who makes you happy. When you find happiness in doing what you love, the people will fall into place with it. When I was going through my divorce, it seemed like everything in my life was turned upside down. I had no idea what direction to go or what was about to become of me. I signed up for college with no idea how I was going to pay for it or who was going to watch my child when I went to class. It worked out. I don't know how, I don't know why, I never had a plan, it just worked out. I knew I needed to do something to make myself feel better and to help better the future of me and my child. I left work on a lunch break, went to the local college, told them I wanted to register, and signed up for an evening English class. I was older than the rest of the students, I had a child, I had my own home and bills to pay, and I felt very out of place. But, surviving that class led to other evening classes. That led to my applying for the licensed practical nursing program because it was shorter than the RN program. That led to quitting my full-time job and finding two part-time jobs. That led to my becoming an LPN. Nursing school also led me to twenty-three other people, during one of the loneliest times of my life, trying to accomplish the same thing I was and nights we all gathered at my house and studied together. When we graduated, we gathered at my house and celebrated together. I obtained an LPN certification and made new friends because I was unsettled one day and decided to take an English class. My daughter sat in the audience and watched as I gave the speech at graduation as the vice president of my nursing class. Short-term goals often lead to long-term happiness. Start small and work your way to bigger and better.

Let go of insecurity. Do not look to others for approval. I swear I could have saved myself from failing at a million things if I had gotten rid of my lack of confidence years ago. If there are a hundred people in a room, ninety of them know about as much as you do. Be the one to speak out. Be the one to say that doesn't make sense to me, help me understand. Be the one to introduce yourself and start a conversation with someone around you. There will be eighty-nine other people who will be glad you did.

Other people don't make the rules for your life. You do. I have mentioned previously that I was less than welcomed with open arms to the small town that I moved to in Tennessee. People who grew up there tended to stay there. Everyone seemed to be connected or have history with everyone else, except me. I can't tell you how many times I heard that if I didn't like it there, leave. The social circles were small and not very inviting. After a few years, I quit focusing my time on the small town and started focusing my time on the hospital that I worked at one town over in the same county. I participated in the hospital activities and tried to be social with everyone in my department. I helped plan nurses' week and 'trunk or treats' and eventually sat on the planning committee for the hospital, which led to my getting invitations to participate in other things. So, as I sat by a campfire one evening in the town I lived in and everyone was teaching me what the phrase "she is just common" means, I brought up the fact that I had been invited to join the county's Junior Auxiliary Chapter. I can't say that I didn't enjoy the shock on everyone's face. One of the ladies exclaimed that she had lived in the town for thirty years and had never been invited to be a part of the JA. She questioned how I got invited. I just smiled and responded that I wasn't sure it was a good fit for me, but I was going to attend the meet-and-greet the following week and see what I thought. I didn't join, but I did get invited back the next year, and I got a little satisfaction from hanging the invitation on my fridge for a while for all my guests to see. It didn't make me famous, but it did remind me that there was someone that wanted me to be a part of their circle.

If you are not welcomed into someone's circle, expand to a bigger circle. The people who are in it for the true meaning and benefit of the group or community as a whole will welcome you. The insecure people who have nothing else to focus on will try to shut you out so you don't steal their thunder. Let them have it and move on to something bigger. The larger the thundercloud then the louder the bang will be.

Know when to stop something that is hurting to you. I can't change my past, but I can change what my daughter is exposed to. The memories and feelings I harbor from dysfunction stop with me. She doesn't have to be exposed to them. I may have lived in an abusive home, but she didn't. She lives in a home that is welcoming and safe. We currently have one of her friends living with us, I refer to her as my love child, and I am so positive that they feel so content at home that I am not sure that I will get neither of them to move out of the house in the near future. I don't tolerate negativity in my house. I don't condone drugs and violence. I don't entertain fear. I took all the things that I felt were negative when I was growing up and made it a point to try to avoid those things. I let people know what I will not tolerate and do not want my child exposed to. She doesn't know a lot about my childhood. I probably will never encourage her to read this book. But I have provided her the childhood that I wanted. Be the person that stops the cycle. My daughter knows that my brother is schizophrenic. Has she ever had to sit and watch one of his manic episodes? No. Her father and I are divorced, but she has never seen or heard us have an argument. Does that mean that he and I have always agreed? No. Have enough backbone to stand up for what you feel is right and no less. Don't wait for someone to change things for you. Change them yourself. You deserve no less.

Be of service to your fellow man. Always speak to someone with an open heart. When you say good morning to someone, say it with a smile and mean it. When you hug someone, squeeze. When you see someone in need, help them without making them feel less. There have been times in my life when I was unsure of how I was going to pay the next bill that was due, but I bought someone groceries on my credit card. There have been times when my credit card was maxed, so I rounded up stuff from my home and left it on the doorstep of someone in need. One day I was in the grocery store and saw two ladies with pen and paper figuring up what they could afford. I dropped my grocery money in their cart and walked out. My family ate grilled cheese sandwiches that night, and we were happy about it. I don't tell you this to brag on myself. I share this because I use to be a person who focused on me, and when I learned to focus on others a little more, my problems seemed to grow smaller.

There is nothing more rewarding than helping someone. Make it a point to spend one day with not yourself, but those around you, in mind and see how you feel at the end of the day. Don't do it for the recognition. Do your good deeds in secret and with a giving heart and you will feel totally different about a lot of things. One of the best rewards I have ever received came when I was standing in line at a store one day behind a man counting his change to pay for an item, and my-ten-year-old daughter whispered in my ear, "Mama, can we help him?" That is the same child I watched count out part of her graduation money to give a friend at school who did not have money to buy his senior portraits of him receiving his diploma. That is also the same child who organized a clean-up day with her classmates at the local battered women's shelter. There is always someone who is carrying a heavier load than you; recognize it and help. You will be surprised how much it lessens the load you are carrying.

Don't be so hard on yourself and let yourself be loved. There is nothing greater in the world than being loved. When someone loves you, accept it and embrace it. Soak it up. Receive it and feel worthy. In everything you do, give and be loved. In someone's worst of times, simply say you are going to love them through it. In everything that surrounds you, create love. Give yourself room for mistakes, own them, and move on. We are all tarnished in some way, yet we all deserve love. When you feel like you are failing, someone is admiring you. When you feel like you are alone, someone is missing you. When you are struggling and can't figure out what to do next, God is molding you. Your misfortune or mistakes could be someone else's lesson that saves them from going through what you are. The world is huge and full of endless possibilities. You may meet someone who tears you down today, but there may be someone else who is your saving grace tomorrow. Your current friends may not be so good for or to you, but your future friends may be amazing. Don't focus on your past or what obstacles you are facing currently. Focus on the future and all the possibilities that await you.

The girl that used to hide under her bedsheets and pray that God would take her to Heaven doesn't feel like a thousand years on this earth would now be enough. The girl who returned from Saudi Arabia during Desert Shield–Desert Storm with not one family member to greet her when she stepped off the plane has a beautiful family sitting on the bench cheering and clapping for her as she muddles her way through a coed softball game. The girl who never thought she was good enough to deserve love has a husband and daughter who wait for her to come home every day. The girl who was molested and lived in a world of abuse as a child now has a safe, warm home where others love to gather. The girl with the big imagination who dreamed of the life she longed for now wouldn't trade places with any other person on earth. The girl that thought no man could be trusted, has a husband the will stick by her and keep trying for the sake of love and what she needs. I will probably deal with my "curse" for the rest of my life, but now sometimes I entertain it instead of letting it control me. I am still not sure where I will end up in this world, but I do know I will end up there with more confidence and more peace than I ever thought I would find.

Thank you for taking time to read my story. I wrote it down in the hopes that it may help someone who feels alone or unworthy. I still feel that I am far from where I am meant to be in this life, but I am happy and mentally healthier than I have ever been. If you feel lost or helpless, please reach out to someone. Don't give up. Your future is counting on you and your story. Make it a happy ending for yourself and your loved ones, even if you haven't met them yet. May you find peace in your darkest moment knowing that you have the strength to overcome whatever hardship you are be called to face and realize that tomorrow, next week, or next year that hardship will be in the past. This world is counting on you to make a difference. You are or will be someone's saving grace. Don't let them miss out…

SWEET CHILD

Say your soul is dark sweet child and your worth is covered with shadows of shame,

Say you can't look into another's eyes and smile for fear they will not do the same.

Say your heart is shattered and your innocence stolen from your overly creative little mind,

Say you can't overcome your fears and peace is not in reach for your soft little hands to find.

Say you make excuses to hide your reality because no one would dare to understand,

Say you live in solitude for fear of rejection and you and loneliness walk hand in hand.

Say you weren't created for this world and you don't have a place to feel free,

Say your mind is controlled by thoughts of others opinions and the condemnation you feel will never flee.

Say your childhood was stolen at the hands of someone you trusted and shared your love,

Say your words are kept silent because you were instructed it was something you could never speak of.

Say your carefree moments were robbed and replaced with feelings of dirtiness and gloom,

Say you want to give up because your value was taken from you way too soon.

Know this sweet child, you are not at fault for the actions of someone controlled by a demon soul,

Although your innocence you can never reclaim, you are still a beautiful creation complete and whole.

There will be days you can't erase from your mind the tainted stains you may feel,

But one day you will find the courage and possess the strength you need to cope and start to heal.

You are destined for great things yet to come and your soul one day you will restore,

You will regain your own beautiful magic and find the peace you are searching for.

-Autumn

ACKOWLEDGMENTS

My life is full of so many people that I owe so much gratitude.

Raquel Waters, you are my peacemaker that tries to find the good in everything. You are the one that can accept things that I have a hard time letting be. Our daughters have been best friends since elementary school and we formed a friendship thru them. We are probably two of the most opposite people you will ever meet in some ways, and yet it seems we are the same. We have supported each other and our children thru many life events. We have shared our children for summer vacations and celebrated their high school graduation's together by taking them on a cruise. Although at times our views may be totally opposite, we share a connection that feeds off of each other and an understanding of one another. There is no question if one will be there for the other because we just know that we will be.

Jennifer Troope, you are my sounding board and usually up for any crazy idea I have with the willingness to add to its craziness. We sit and I can talk for hours while you listen with all your attention and I can see my emotions reflecting in your face. I can call you when I am having a bad day and vent for a couple of minutes, hang up the phone and you will act like that is a normal thing to do. We work at the same hospital and are usually found having our lunch together every day. When we sit down, we know how each other's days are going just by the look on our faces. If I want to go get doughnuts in my pajamas, then you think that is the grandest idea ever. If I wanted to rob a bank, you would probably tell me I was crazy as you are getting your mask ready to go. If I tell you I am having a gathering, you make the list of necessities and arrive early to help me prepare for it. I have watched you over the years raise your daughter alone with such grace that it makes being a single mom look easy. I have seen you mow your grass, paint your cabinets, and make a home for you and your child. And I have seen you the day after you did manual labor at home when you show up at work dressed to perfection and presenting yourself as nothing but professional. Often times I don't think you even realize the strength you carry inside yourself or give yourself enough credit, and that draws me to you even more.

Rena Hart, you have been my friend since my Georgia days. Although you now live in Florida and I in Tennessee, we are still as close as we ever were. You carry in you the magic that overtakes people when they are near you and peace can be felt. We have our Saturday or Sunday morning phone conversations while sharing our morning coffee and we try to meet up for summer vacations. There has never been a loss with our connection no matter the distance in our physical locations. You are my always was and forever will be friend. You are an old soul that can rationalize and explain and give direction from the heart.

Kimberly and Bryant Workman, you are our laughing friends. I don't care what we are doing it is going to be funny. Even if it is not funny, it will be to us. We have shed many tears from laughing at the simplest of things we do together. We have packed up and went out of town for a trip and ended up staying in the hotel room entertaining ourselves more than going out and exploring. You are the ones that we can spend an entire evening riding back roads and getting out of the vehicle at random stops and have a dance off in the headlights. You are the ones that I really can't pinpoint when the friendship begun, it was just there naturally when we met each other.

Chad and Dawn Hollis, you are the friends that are also our family. Chad, you have been a friend to my husband since you were in elementary school, and you have been a friend to me since the first day I met you. We have shared divorce, death, and many shortcomings together. We see the ugly in each other's lives and still get involved and can be counted on to help. You are the get up in the middle of the night and drive 800 miles to change our car tire friends. We will fight like brothers and sisters one day, but you can count on us to be there the next day. We eat Sunday dinner together as often as we can and have shared many Christmas' and

Thanksgivings and Birthday parties that it was just us and it was nothing short of the feeling of family.

Dustin and Samantha Wright, you are our neighbors that we count on for the stuff we need to borrow or to drop by the house and make sure everything is alright. We share a driveway and our lives to add to our safe havens. We have watched and participated in each other's lives and our children share the same spot of the world that they call home. It is a given that we will be there for one another.

Alan and Kathy Kennedy, you have provided us a home away from home when we visit Georgia. We have shared business trips, celebrated our kid's accomplishments together, and spent many nights laughing while arguing our way thru a good game of spades. You two have no idea of the love we have for you and will always carry.

Amy Williams, you have filled so many shoes throughout my life. You have been my cousin, my sister, and my best friend. You always said you admired me for leaving and doing things outside of our small town, but I admire you way more for staying and building the family that you have. You are always there for me and my go to person for about anything. I love you dearly and could never repay you or explain to you what you mean to me. You are a beautiful soul inside and out.

Samantha and Curtis, Justin Robinette, T-Bone, Tracy Hickman, Freda Bennett, Laura Turner, Dr. Clarke, Dr. Peters and there are so many more that makes my life complete and brings happiness into my world. All I can say to each one of you is Thank You!

My husband and daughter, there are not enough words. Just, I love you to sum it all up. Thank you for dealing with me and being mine.